The Foster Parenting Manual

of related interest

Foster Parenting Step-by-Step
How to Nurture the Traumatized Child and Overcome Conflict
Dr. Kalyani Gopal
ISBN 978 1 84905 937 4
eISBN 978 0 85700 751 3

Life Story Work with Children Who are Fostered or Adopted
Creative Ideas and Activities
Katie Wrench and Lesley Naylor
ISBN 978 1 84905 343 3
eISBN 978 0 85700 674 5

Why Can't my Child Behave?
Empathic Parenting Strategies that Work for Adoptive and Foster Families
Amber Elliott
ISBN 978 1 84905 339 6
eISBN 978 0 85700 671 4

Attachment in Common Sense and Doodles
A Practical Guide
Miriam Silver
Doodles by Teg Lansdell
ISBN 978 1 84905 314 3
eISBN 978 0 85700 624 0

Inside Transracial Adoption
Strength-based, Culture-sensitizing Parenting Strategies for Inter-
country or Domestic Adoptive Families That Don't "Match"
2nd edition
Beth Hall and Gail Steinberg
ISBN 978 1 84905 905 3
eISBN 978 0 85700 651 6

Welcoming a New Brother or Sister Through Adoption
From Navigating New Relationships to Building a Loving Family
Arleta James
Foreword by Gregory C. Keck, PhD.
ISBN 978 1 84905 903 9
eISBN 978 0 85700 653 0

Reparenting the Child Who Hurts
A Guide to Healing Developmental Trauma and Attachments
Caroline Archer and Christine Gordon
Foreword by Gregory C. Keck, PhD.
ISBN 978 1 84905 263 4
eISBN 978 0 85700 568 7

Creating Loving Attachments
Parenting with PACE to Nurture Confidence and Security in the Troubled Child
Kim S. Golding and Daniel A. Hughes
ISBN 978 1 84905 227 6
eISBN 978 0 85700 470 3

The Foster Parenting

MANUAL

A Practical Guide to Creating a Loving, Safe and Stable Home

John DeGarmo

Foreword by Mary Perdue

Jessica Kingsley *Publishers*
London and Philadelphia

First published in 2013
by Jessica Kingsley Publishers
116 Pentonville Road
London N1 9JB, UK
and
400 Market Street, Suite 400
Philadelphia, PA 19106, USA

www.jkp.com

Library of Congress Cataloging in Publication Data
DeGarmo, John, 1969-
  The foster parenting manual : a practical guide to creating a loving, safe
and stable home / John DeGarmo ; foreword by Mary Perdue.
    pages cm
  Includes index.
  ISBN 978-1-84905-956-5
  1. Foster parents. 2. Foster children. 3. Parenting. I. Title.
  HQ759.7.D44 2013
  306.874--dc23
                              2013012292

British Library Cataloguing in Publication Data
A CIP catalogue record for this book is available from the British Library

ISBN 978 1 84905 956 5
eISBN 978 0 85700 795 7

Printed and bound in Great Britain by Bell & Bain ltd., Glasgow

For Cassie and Brailey, who continue
to remind me that the need is strong

"For I was hungry, and you gave me something to eat; I was thirsty, and you gave me something to drink; I was a stranger, and you took me in."

Matthew 25:35

Contents

Foreword

For the vast majority of people in our culture today, the world of foster care is mysterious, frightening, and repelling. The cloud of uncertainty and fear that surrounds the foster care system is due in large part to the fact that most people are unacquainted with this system, or anyone within this system. Their perspectives are clouded by their lack of accurate information. Their emotions are seared by what they read or see in the media, which invariably is an instance of further abuse or neglect of a child in state custody, or even more tragically, of death occurring while a child is in care. Therefore, we come to this subject with misperceptions and jaded views because we know of the failings of our culture to protect every child, to ensure that every single child is loved, nurtured, and reared to be a productive adult.

What is the mission of the foster care system? It is, at its core, the protection of children within our society. Most of us as "average people" are repulsed by the thought that a parent could harm their child. We are angered by the notion that adults do not care for their own, that addictions and greed, the problems that plague our society on the whole, have somehow filtered down to the innocent, the "least of these," the most vulnerable in our world. We don't want to see what has happened; we don't want to know about this most horrific problem in our civilized society. Yet the need is great and very real. Adults, for a myriad of reasons, find themselves unable or unwilling to care for their children in positive ways. This is when the government comes into the picture, to rescue the little ones and provide stability, safety, and the basics of life. Enter the foster parent...

Dr. John DeGarmo paints an accurate and compelling picture of the life of a foster family, the parents, children, and caseworkers involved in providing safety, love, encouragement, and stability for children in crisis. Each chapter of this book opens with a true story from foster parents about their experiences while on this amazing journey we call fostering. Dr. DeGarmo doesn't minimize the frustrations and difficulties of becoming a foster parent; rather, he provides calm assurance that though problems are sure to come, they are not insurmountable in most cases. While foster children inevitably arrive with their own emotional and sometimes physical trauma, consistent and loving parenting provides the healing balm for their young lives. Children tend to be resilient beyond what we adults can imagine. Impacting their present circumstances ensures their futures will be brighter, healthier, and more successful.

Dr. DeGarmo is clear in his message to prospective foster parents: the job is not an easy one and should not be undertaken lightly. He writes with compassion from his personal experience in fostering over 30 children through the years. He trains foster parents and speaks to foster parenting groups routinely in an effort to educate the public and provide support to those considering the call to foster. This book provides much-needed insight and clarity into an issue shadowed by a lack of accurate information. It is a long-awaited primer on the basics of fostering.

Thank you, Dr. John DeGarmo, for providing from your pool of experiences the incentive to become involved. This involvement is the only thing that will preserve our foster care system for the good of children in need.

Mary Perdue
First Lady of Georgia,
January 2003–January 2011

Acknowledgments

As I documented countless times in my first book, *Fostering Love: One Foster Parent's Journey*, I could never be a foster parent without the many people who have helped out my family in a number of ways. This is true with this book, as well. There are so many people that have helped with this book that it is impossible to name them all. I would, though, like to thank those who so kindly shared their personal insights as a foster parent and foster friend.

Introduction

As I was writing my doctoral dissertation on responding to the needs of foster children in public schools, a study I hoped would help foster parents and caseworkers aid foster children as they struggle greatly in our schools, I realized that there was not much information or resources for new foster parents. Along with this, I also discovered that there simply were not many resources for foster parents, in general. As one who has fostered over three dozen children during the past 12 years, this affected my family, as well, if we were to continue looking after these children in need in a healthy fashion.

The knowledge of this discovery was only strengthened as I spoke to foster parent associations at various training sessions and conferences across the nation. During my many training sessions with foster parents, both new to the system and veterans, it became more and more apparent that educational information for foster parents is difficult to come by. I had the fortune to speak with many foster parents, listening to their questions and their concerns. I heard how they could not find the help they needed. I also heard how they could not find the support from within their own community. Indeed, the general public has very little information or insight about foster care, and this lack of knowledge carries through into all aspects of foster care. Thus, the necessity for this book came about.

The Foster Parenting Manual: A Practical Guide to Creating a Loving, Safe and Stable Home is a book that is written for those who are involved with the foster care system. Whether you are a foster parent, or caseworker, this book will be an asset to you. *The Foster Parenting Manual* is designed to offer insight into the entire foster care system. In short, it is a manual for those who are courageous enough to look after those children who are in desperate need, our foster children.

Each chapter begins with a personal observation about the chapter's topic from a foster parent, or one who has worked with foster parents. These personal observations offer insight into the foster care system from those who have lived it on a day-to-day basis, and who have experienced the joys, the sorrows, and the challenges of working with foster children. By reading through these observations, you will be able to gain valuable insight into fostering beyond what any training session or publication might offer.

Perhaps you have been a foster parent for some time now, or perhaps you are preparing to take your first foster child into your home. *The Foster Parenting Manual* is a book that you can pick up time and time again and refer to it, as the information contained in this book will be helpful to the veteran foster parent, or the beginner. After all, each time a new foster child comes into your home, you are certain to meet with new challenges, as each placement is unique, just as the child is.

Thank you for what you do. Thank you for being a foster parent and caring for children. Sadly the need is strong, as there are so many children placed into care each year. Yet there are so few willing to be a foster parent, as it is not an easy task. Truly, it is the hardest job you will ever come to love.

For the children,
Dr. John N. DeGarmo

Note: For ease of reading, the male pronoun has been used to refer to the hypothetical child throughout, while the female pronoun has been used to refer to the hypothetical caregiver and caseworker. Names in all case studies have been changed to preserve anonymity.

CHAPTER 1

Foster Care

Children, Parents, and Caseworkers

Mandy and Ray, foster parents of 13 years

I had always looked at foster children as something very unusual, very strange. I didn't really know what a foster child was, other than a child who was, for some reason, taken away from his or her parents. I suppose I thought they had caused enough trouble that they had to be placed into a foster home, and that they were to blame.

As for foster parents, well, I had a different opinion of them; they were unusual, strange, and even a little weird. After all, who would take children into their own home that didn't belong to them, children who were most probably troubled? They must be special people, I thought, people with a great deal of patience and a great deal of love.

As I began to raise my own children, I found that my compassion for children in need became stronger, week by week, and day by day. I wanted to dearly protect my own children from anything that might harm them. I became upset when I saw injustices done to other children. My heart sank when I read of other children hurt by others, or worse. I wanted to help protect children from harm, to reach out and shield those children from hostile and damaging environments. But what could I do?

When I visited the county fair with my family one fall afternoon, I came across a booth filled with information about being a foster parent. I spoke with some of the foster parent volunteers there, and went home, not giving it any further thought. Yet, I suppose a seed was planted in the back of my brain. Over the course of the next week, I thought a lot about foster parenting. The foster parents I met at the county fair seemed nice, pleasant, and even sane. They spoke of helping children in need; they talked about opening up their homes to children who needed a stable home; they shared with me the fact that foster children mainly needed a family to look after them and to love them. Maybe this was the way I could help children. But, it sure seemed like a huge commitment.

After talking with my husband, we decided to open up our own home as a foster home. Our two beautiful children were excited to have other children in their home with them, and told us they would help by being a big sister and a big brother to them. After the training was complete, we took our first foster child into our home, a three-year-old boy who was neglected by his parents. He was hungry, he was beaten, he was sad, and he was scared. Many months went by, and our three-year-old became just like a member of our own family, as my husband and I grew to love him. Our own children were wonderful as they helped him with learning how to speak, how to eat, and even how to dress. Perhaps the most important thing they did for him was to treat him like a valued equal, including him in all that they did. It took a while, but he learned how to smile, and his laugh was like medicine for our whole family.

He has since gone back home to live with his family, and even though we don't know what his future might be, we pray we have planted a seed in him, seeds of love, compassion, and hope. As I look back upon the many foster children who have come through our doors, I realize that foster parents are simply people who have a love for children, and who have a desire to help change the world, one child at a time.

Being a foster parent might just be the hardest thing you ever do. Yet, being a foster parent might also be the most rewarding mission you ever undertake, as well. There are those who say that foster parenting is "heart work," as it is a job that takes a great deal of commitment from your heart. There will be moments when you are exhausted, worn out, and frustrated. At the same time, there will be those moments when you are filled with laughter, joy, and love. Foster parenting will bring you all of these emotions, and so much more.

Perhaps you have the desire to help out children who suffer from abuse or neglect. Maybe you feel compassion for children who face malnutrition or even drug-related problems passed on from a mother's addiction. Possibly, your heart goes out to those children who are rejected by those who were supposed to love them most: their parents. After all, you feel that every child deserves the right to be in a healthy and supportive home, and most importantly, every child deserves to be loved unconditionally. As a foster parent, you have the opportunity to help these children in need. When you foster a child, not only do you invest in the future and well-being of a child, you are also changing the life of that child.

What is Foster Care?

Foster care is a form of placement for children who are in need of being placed in a home or environment outside of their home of origin. This placement is a 24-hour substitute care for these children, while they are placed outside their own home. A child is often placed into foster care when a state's child protection agency determines that the home the child is living in is no longer a safe environment. After this determination has been made by a state, a judge must agree to this, signing all necessary paperwork in order for a child to be removed, and placed into foster care, accordingly. During the time a foster child is placed in a foster home, the birth family is assigned a case plan. Each case plan is different, according to the challenges that the family faces, according to the reasons the child is placed into foster care. It is the goal of each case plan for a foster child to be reunited with the birth family or family members. This reunification occurs when the family has concluded the obligations of their case plan. Many courts allow a family one year to conclude the case plan. If a family is unable to meet the demands expected of them in the case plan after a court-appointed time, the family may lose their permanent custody of the child.

As foster care is intended to be a temporary placement, the time frame in a foster home varies from one foster child to the next, with some staying only one day and others staying as long as a couple of years. The average amount of time a foster child spends in the United States foster care system is 28.6 months in length, with half of all foster children being placed in another home for a year or more (DeGarmo 2012a). As a result, most of these children have not experienced a stable or nurturing environment during their early, formative years. Again, the length of time spent in a foster home is different for each child, dependent upon the child's situation. As a foster parent, you may never really know how long a foster child will stay in your house. A foster child may stay in your house for a day or for a year. One of the emotional challenges you will face as a foster parent is the uncertainty of the placement, and at times, the sad timing of a reunification with a foster child's birth family.

Who are Foster Children?

Foster care is available for any child between the ages of birth until 18 years of age. When a child reaches the age of 18, most will exit the foster system. The average age of a child in custody is 10.2 years. Of all children in foster care, 47 percent of these are in their teens. When a child is placed in custody under foster care, and into your foster home, the intention is for the child to eventually be reunited with his or her birth family. Roughly six out of every ten children placed in foster care are reunited with birth parents or family members (DeGarmo 2012a).

Children are placed under foster care for a number of reasons. Many of these reasons overlap, with the child suffering from numerous mental and emotional challenges. These reasons may include one or more of the following:

- *Neglect*: A child may be neglected in a number of ways. A parent may neglect a child's basic need for food. Sanitary living conditions may be neglected, leaving a child in an unsanitary household. The lack of proper and needed medical conditions can also be a symptom of neglect. Children may face neglect due to lack of supervision, placing the child in an unsafe environment. Finally, many foster children suffer from emotional neglect, as their emotional needs have not been met by a parent or adult.

- *Physical abuse*: Abuse takes many forms. One of these is abuse through a physical injury caused by a parent or caregiver. Physical abuse may take many forms, with the severity of the injury sustained ranging from a visible bruising to a more tragic situation where the parent or caregiver physically assaults the child. Physical abuse can even take the form of locking a child in a closet or other confined space. Many times, the child welfare agency works with the parents in an attempt to help them learn alternate methods of discipline. But, when these methods fail, and a child is being abused, the state steps in, removing the child from the household.

- *Sexual abuse*: Disturbingly, sexual abuse may take several different forms. Sexual abuse of a child may involve voyeurism, the viewing of pornographic material or sexual acts with a child, or the act of sexual fondling, penetration or rape of a child.

- *Parental drug/alcohol abuse*: Those parents who abuse drugs and/or alcohol place their children in danger. This danger may result in neglect, physical abuse, or domestic violence.

- *Child drug/alcohol abuse*: Those parents who allow their child to take drugs and/or alcohol also place their children in danger. Parents may either ignore the danger or be unaware of the child's abuse of the drugs/alcohol.

- *Domestic violence*: When a child is living in an environment where two or more caregivers are engaged in a violent altercation, the child's safety is then jeopardized through this violence.

- *Inadequate housing*: When a parent is no longer able to provide a clean, safe, healthy environment for a child, the child is removed and placed into foster care. Many times, these children are homeless.

- *Incarceration*: Children may be placed into foster care after all parents, family members, and caregivers are unavailable due to their placement into prison, or jail.

- *Death*: On very rare occasions, a parent's death leads to a situation where there are no family members willing, able, or available to provide and care for a child.

- *Abandonment*: Abandonment occurs when a parent or caregiver chooses to leave the child voluntarily. Many times, this abandonment may occur with a friend, neighbor, or a baby-sitter. Other times, a parent may simply leave the child at home for a great length of time.

Placement in the foster care system takes many forms. Some children may live with foster parents unrelated to them, while other children may live with relatives temporarily or with family members intent upon adopting the child. Over two million children live with family members or in group homes outside of the foster care system, or even in an intensive form known as Treatment Foster Care, which provides therapeutic treatment services.

Foster Parents

Foster parents are those people who open their homes to foster children in an attempt to assist troubled children. They are just like you; they have a desire to help children in need. These licensed caregivers must go through a number of hours of training, attend orientation meetings, have their homes approved by the agency, and obtain a criminal background check. Each country (and, within the US, each state) has different rules, guidelines, expectations, and laws. The number of foster children living within a foster home depends upon several factors. These may include the size of the foster home, the number of bedrooms within the home, how many children live in the home, the maximum number of children allowed in the home by the state's standards, and quite simply, the enthusiasm and energy of the foster family. As a foster parent, you may merely be too tired to take in more than a certain number.

A successful foster parent is one who provides a caring environment while a birth family works on their caseload for reunification. Foster parents not only provide a caring environment, but a safe and stable one, as well. During this time, as a foster parent, you will agree to carry out all functions of the birth family. These day-to-day functions include assuring that the child's medical, nutritional, educational, and parental needs are met. Foster parents may also provide social activities for the child, as well, such as extra-curricular events after school, city and county sports, and faith-related activities, to name a few.

Those foster programs within the United States that are sponsored by state child welfare programs do allocate a monthly stipend to help with the cost of taking another child into a home. Each child is allocated a certain amount, depending upon the child's age, as well as the state's allotment. This money is to cover food, clothing, and personal allowance. Some states also provide a small allotment for special occasions, such as birthday and Christmas. Medical care is also provided by the government. Each child receives a state medical card, guaranteeing that payment for all medical needs, along with necessary medicines, are met. Foster parents should not pay for a medical bill, directly out of their own savings. The same system works in government-sponsored foster care programs in Australia, and in many European nations, as well.

Caseworkers

A caseworker is an employee of the child welfare agency who is assigned to the foster child, generally for the entire time the child is placed under the care of the agency. Caseworkers will work in conjunction with the state, as well as the court system, as they place the child into a foster home. The caseworker selects a foster home placement for the child, attempting to find the best suitable home situation for both the foster child and the foster parent. Foster children are often enrolled in a new school when assigned a caseworker to assist them in the foster care process. Eventual reunification with their parents and family is usually the hoped-for goal. Caseworkers are specifically trained to provide mental health relief, as they often work with troubled children. Caseworkers ensure that the medical needs of the child are met.

Caseworkers are required to visit the home of each foster child once a month in an attempt to see how the foster child is progressing, as well as to gather information from the foster parents and answer any questions they might have. Caseworkers also work alongside the child's teachers, therapists, doctors, and any other caregiver. A caseworker will often have to testify in a juvenile court of law in regard to the safety of the home the foster child is placed in, as well as provide information about the child.

Difficult working conditions, poor compensation, larger caseloads due to reductions in staff, and the responsibilities of providing continuous support to the birth parents, foster children, and foster parents result in many caseworkers failing to continue employment in this line of work past the first year. Along with this, caseworkers often deal with children who have serious behavioral problems, and those children who are emotionally depressed due to the situation they are in. Caseworkers may also have to work with angry birth parents who blame the child welfare agency, or even the caseworkers themselves, for the removal of their child, or for their own personal issues.

CHAPTER 2

The History of Foster Care

Frank and Amy, foster parents of nine years

Amy moved into our house when she was seven. Amy was placed in foster care due to neglect. As the seven-year-old lived with her alcoholic grandmother, Amy often had to look after herself: ensure that she had food to eat, make sure she got to and from school, and take care of the house she lived in. When she came to live with us, it was apparent that Amy had no boundaries. She ran wild! Soon, our brand new house was a mess. Newly painted walls were drawn on and the hard wood floors we loved were deeply scratched. School was even more of a challenge. One of us had to visit the school on a weekly basis, as Amy would continuously get into some sort of trouble. On top of that, Amy lied to us on a daily basis. It was as if she didn't know any better.

Yet, our whole family came to love her. Our own children, who were ages seven, five, and four, played with Amy and treated her as if she was one of the family. We even took her on vacation to the mountains with us, one year.

After Amy had lived with us for a year and a half, becoming a dear and important part of our family, she suddenly moved to another state. With very little notice, Amy's grandparents contacted the state's welfare agency, and gained custody of her. On December 23 of that year, Frank packed up Amy's wrapped Christmas presents, along with all of her belongings, and drove her to her new home. Tears flowed from all of us. We were happy for Amy, yet wondered if we would ever see her again.

Three years later, Amy called us on the phone late one evening. She had been placed back into foster care in yet another state, due to physical abuse by her aunt and uncle. We were going on vacation the next day, so we took down the phone number of the foster family she was with. Unfortunately, when we returned and called them back, Amy had been moved yet again. For years, we tried tracking her down, but as each state has a different welfare system, it became impossible to locate any information about her. We are still trying to find her, and hope that one day we can remind her that she is loved by us.

In order to fully understand foster care in the United States, it is necessary to look as far back as the eighteenth century. At that time, local government officials were given the task of distributing relief to the poor and impoverished. Often, these officials were also granted authority to indenture children from families in poverty in lieu of monetary relief. Local officials were to ensure that children were fed, housed, clothed, and provided with the necessary training of skills. As society became more aware of the challenges of underprivileged children, along with the growing number of orphans, orphanages were established.

The early nineteenth century saw the establishment of what grew to become the middle class. At the same time, the conception grew that early childhood was an important and separate part of human development. The character of children was to be shaped by internalizing beliefs of morality and behavior instead of breaking their wills, the prevailing approach in colonial times. The outcome was a change in child-rearing methods, as children began to live longer and stay home for longer periods of time, instead of being forced to enter the workforce at early ages. The early nineteenth century was also a time when children only from low income homes were indentured. Some states were required to furnish children with a minimum of three months of education per year. As states began to wane in indenturing children by the middle of the nineteenth century, religious institutes, along with charitable organizations, began to open their own orphanages.

The year 1853 witnessed a drastic change in regard to orphans and impoverished children. Charles Loring Brace, an austere critic of orphanages and asylums, introduced the idea of placing these children in homes, rather than the traditional orphanage. Brace founded the Children's Aid Society (CAS) later in that year, with the CAS's vision that children should be placed in homes rather than in institutions. It was Brace's personal belief that children should live in rural areas, as he was against city life. As a result, Brace endeavored to place children from urban slums into homes in the country. The year 1873 saw Mary Ellen Wilson enter the scene. This young girl was found by a church worker when she was reported by her neighbors. Young Mary Ellen was bruised, thin, and her skin was caked in dirt. When a New York judge became aware of the situation, Mary Ellen was removed from her home, and placed into another, thus making her the first official foster child.

The later part of the nineteenth century saw an awareness of the importance of social issues, such as child abuse and parental neglect. The Society for the Prevention of Cruelty to Children (SPCC) was created and became active in large eastern cities. Soon, members of the SPCC were granted permission from the courts and began to remove children from abusive and neglectful homes and placed them within other homes and orphan asylums. Families, such as those in Boston, Massachusetts, that took children into their homes, were being paid. With this change in policy in payment to families, child placement agencies began to look more closely at the conditions in the placement homes where children were boarded. The term "foster care" came into fashion, sometimes replacing the phrase "boarding out."

In 1909, the White House Council of Children established a resolution that altered the earlier philosophy and policies in regard to child welfare. This resolution was a new philosophy that held the belief that children needed to be reared in happy and stable environments. Shortly later in 1915, California licensed, as well as regulated, agencies that found placement homes for children. Five years later, the state began to pay these homes for this service.

The Aid to Dependent Children (ADC) Act, which was Title IV of the Social Security Act, gave impoverished families access to federal funds, enabling these families to keep their children at home, rather than have the children placed in orphan asylums.

Furthermore, the ADC with its additional federal funding aided those establishments that housed children taken from their homes. By 1950, more children were in foster homes than in orphanages and other institutions. The number of children in foster homes continued to increase by 1960, as there were twice as many children placed in foster homes than institutions. This number tripled by 1968, and by 1976, the number of children placed into foster homes exceeded 100,000 (U.S. General Accounting Office 1977).

A number of critics harshly criticized the foster care system, declaring that the ease in which children entered into care was troublesome. As a result of their heavy criticism, Congress passed federal foster care legislation, the Adoption Assistance and Child Welfare Act of 1980. This act addressed two critical issues. The first was that states resorted consistently to foster care as a means of intervention in regard to the child's relationship with the family. Second, the government saw placing children into foster care as an answer to the ever-growing dilemma of where to place children living outside of their homes. With this in mind, Congress expected the states to keep children safely in their own homes by using the states' own methods, resources, and other services.

Although the number of foster children placed in homes declined between the 1970s and the early 1980s, the number increased greatly beginning in the mid 1980s. Between 1987 and 1992, the population of foster children went from 280,000 to more than 460,000. In addition, the number of children raised by their grandparents outside of foster care, or children living outside of their birth parents yet in a relative's home, rose from two to three million (Child Welfare League of America 2005). In 1997, Congress passed the Adoption and Safe Families Act (ASFA). AFSA mandated that federal and local officials were responsible in creating a program to focus on the problem of the nation's burgeoning foster care population, and that both federal and local officials were to focus principally on the reduction of time children spent in foster care.

Each state in the United States has different policies and procedures for its foster care system. Indeed, what may be a rule in one state may not be in another. Differences abound between each state in regard to reimbursement, care, and training. Furthermore, states do not communicate efficiently between each other when a child is transferred from one state to another while in foster care. These differences make it difficult for foster parents, foster children, and caseworkers on several levels.

Foster Care Around the World Today

As there are differences in foster care services throughout the United States, it comes as no surprise then that there are also vast and wide differences in the way nations around the world implement their foster care services and agencies. In truth, the term "foster care" is one that has tremendous differences in various areas of the world. In many industrialized nations, foster care commonly refers to a temporary placement, made by a state child welfare agency, with a family. These foster families undergo training by the government, and are closely monitored to ensure the child's safety. Foster families in these industrialized nations are compensated by the state agency, though compensation varies widely from one US state to another, and from one industrialized nation to another. For example, foster families in Australia are paid significantly more than their counterparts in the United States. For many Third World and developing nations, the term "foster care" is one that refers to something that is quite different than the system established in the industrialized nations.

In many developing nations across the globe, poor economic situations leave little financial assistance for government assistance. Lack of available health care, adoption organizations, and governmental aid for families and children are the reality. As a result, foster care agencies are not in place, resulting in many displaced children. Foster care in these parts of the world is much more informal and often unregulated by a state agency. Often, children are placed with family members or even orphanages.

Throughout much of the African continent, the practice of placing underprivileged children into other homes is an old tradition, and not an uncommon one. This practice has been called many things, including adoption, child circulation, child rearing, fosterage, and fostering, with the latter term being the most common one. The use of so many terms creates confusion, and certainly reflects different practices. There are an abundance of reasons why children may be placed in different homes: the death of parents, divorce, illness, separation of family members, and even for the strengthening of family ties through future arranged marriages. Girls are "fostered out" far more than boys are in most African nations. As educational opportunities increase in many African nations, children are also being "fostered out" to other families, families that are closer to large cities where schools are more readily available. Sadly, many children in these countries would not have access to school and educational opportunities if it were not for this type of fostering.

As there is no government financial assistance in these nations, often the foster child is expected, and required, to perform a number of domestic chores around the house as a source of payment or reimbursement to their foster family. For some foster children in this scenario, they are thought of as domestic servants, not children, and are treated in a harsh and even abusive fashion. Large numbers of those "foster children" placed in homes for educational opportunities often fail school, and even drop out, due often to the poor conditions they live in.

As mentioned earlier, the poor economic environment in Africa has severely affected the fostering system. "Child shifting," as fostering is also known, is not financially possible, as families are simply not financially able to take another child into their home. Couple this with the tremendous increase in those children whose parents have died from HIV/AIDS-related diseases, this leads to a large number of orphaned children trying to survive without any assistance, neither from government nor from family members in a form of foster care. Quite simply, the high costs of properly installing an effective foster care system prohibit many African countries from developing it.

For the millions of orphan children in Asian countries, the foster care system offers little hope. Families are a deep cornerstone for many Asian countries, and children are highly valued. Fortunately, many children whose parents have died find outside parental care with extended family members, in a form of kinship living arrangement, a type of family preservation service. For some Asian nations, this is the only option that is supported by the government. As a result, millions of children who have no living extended family member find themselves without a home. More often than not, Asian governments are quick to place a child into an orphanage. The majority of these orphanages are overcrowded, understaffed, with children living in poor conditions. For those children not living in an orphanage or in kinship care, they turn to the streets, where too often violence awaits them. HIV/AIDS-related diseases are prevalent among children living in these situations.

Foster care was first introduced in Japan shortly after World War II, partly in response to the large number of orphaned children. Some 60-plus years later, the foster care system is one that is seldom used, with only 6 percent of children in need placed in a foster home (Thoburn 2007). Japan's culture may be an explanation for this low number. "Family" typically is constrained to the strict ties of tradition of blood and marriage. For those children who fall outside these cultural traditions, it is often difficult for them to find a home that is welcoming. Disturbingly, Japan's culture is one that is resistant to foster children, as there is a lack of understanding from all portions of its society. Another struggle that foster children face in Japan is the lack of aftercare provisions. For those children who have aged out of the foster care system, they have little to no support, and often are completely on their own.

European countries are generally considered to have the most advanced foster care systems available. However, there are distinct differences between regions throughout the continent. In the Nordic, or Scandinavian, nations, the system is perhaps the most efficient and advanced. The governments of these nations are very involved in the promotion of foster care, and provide sufficient funds, staff, and training. Western European nations have seen a reduction of government involvement in foster care, though it is still a highly developed child welfare system. The lack of funds has seen a large decrease in the placement of children into care. Central and Eastern European nations have the weakest foster care system and the lowest number of foster homes on the continent. Nevertheless, this region has the greatest need for a foster care system, as more children are in need of placement into a foster home than in any other region of Europe.

Efforts are under way to bring about social change in a global foster care system. Organizations, such as the International Foster Care Organization (IFCO), are working hard to bring about a more unified way to support foster children around the world. Yet, there is much work to be done, as the foster care system is drastically uneven across the four corners of the globe. All children, regardless of where they are born, have the right to a loving home, a supportive family, and a stable environment. An improved global foster care system will help to make that dream a reality for millions of children.

CHAPTER 3

Training

Lori and Brett, foster parents of two years

I walked out of yet another fertility office visit crying, wondering how to tell my husband that once again the medication did not work. I looked up and there was a sign that said "foster to adopt." I had always talked with my husband about fostering to adopt. I knew the talk would be hard but I also knew that fertility was harder. That ride back home was a long one as I cried, praying for the right way to start the talk.

We went to a training session in January. Brett sounded like he might have changed his mind about foster to adopt. He was reading a lot about foster parents and looking at what to expect when fostering. We looked at adoptable children and even talked to other foster parents about it to see if it was right for us. The following January, we signed up for the classes and took them and met all kinds of fellow future foster parents. The last night as I walked out to the truck, I felt like I was one step closer to my Brady bunch family of my dreams. I had finished everything. I painted the rooms and ordered bunk beds and a dresser. I even had clothes and toys ready and waiting. Dreaming of more kids in the house, I made sure everything was perfect in the rooms down to the pictures on the walls. Things in our own life were changing, too. My own son Adam started first grade, and my father became ill in September, so we once again put the fostering to adopt off until he got better.

Finally, in November, we had our first placement, a beautiful little boy who was four and a red-haired little girl who was three. I was so happy to get the call I said yes without thinking. The caseworker got to the house around nine that night, and the children were scared and sleepy. The little girl had been through a horrible ordeal. She had bruises from head to toe, had not been washed in ages, and was wearing clothes that smelled horrible. Being a loving mother, I could never picture anyone doing this to a sweet angel. I had to walk out of the bathroom to keep from crying in front of the small bruised girl sitting in the tub of water.

The next few days revealed many shocking stories from the children. Beatings from family members, lack of food, neglect; the shock of these stories still lives with me today. Birthdays came and the children were so happy to have parties of their own. I could not help but go all out with the thought being that they may never have another birthday party. I wanted it to be special for them and something to remember in the future. Their eyes lit up like stars in the sky, and I knew deep down that I would have no problem loving these angels.

If I could give a word of advice for a first-time foster family, it would be prayer, hope, and understanding. It is hard, and there are no easy ways out. You will find yourself dealing with parents, counselors, and caseworkers, some of whom will have different ideas on child raising. I would not change anything I have done for these children.

Making the decision to be a foster parent is a difficult one. It takes incredible commitment, unconditional love, and patience. After you determine that you are ready to begin, there are long hours of training ahead of you before your first foster child is placed in your home, and becomes part of your family. These hours of training will go a long way in helping you prepare for the many challenges that await you as a foster parent.

Whether you are fostering in the United States or in another country, each organization has its own set of laws and policies in regard to foster parent training. Thus, your situation will probably be different from somebody else who lives in a neighboring state. The first step is to locate your city's child welfare agency, and contact them. Perhaps you already know someone who is a foster parent, and they can help you find the correct contact information. If so, you are one step ahead. If not, the phone book or internet is a great way to find what you are looking for. As each state is different, you will find that there are a number of different names for child welfare agencies. In the Resources at the end of this book you will find a list of each state's child welfare agency and contact information.

Before contacting the agency nearest to you, it is important to determine whether you qualify as a possible foster parent, as there are requirements to be met before you become certified. These include the following:

- *Age*: Foster parents need to be at least 21 years of age in order to begin taking foster children into their homes.

- *Character*: Character references are necessary in many occupations, including fostering children. You must have three signed statements from individuals stating that you have strong moral character, are able to develop meaningful relationships with children, can effectively manage financially, and have sound judgment.

- *Financial*: Though you will be reimbursed for having a foster child placed in your home, the daily reimbursement fee is small, and differs from state to state. Before a foster child is placed in your home, you may be asked to show that you are financially stable enough to support another child.

- *Health*: Having a foster child in your house can be draining, emotionally, mentally, and physically. In order to have a child placed in your home, each member of your family must be in mental and physical health. This includes no drug or alcohol abuse. You, and each member of your household, will have to have a medical examination, and a physical report from your doctor will have to be turned into the child welfare agency, and kept on file.

- *Marital status*: As each state is different, your marital status may be a factor in your certification as a foster parent. If you are married, you will have to have a copy of your marriage certificate turned into the child welfare agency, and kept on file. If your status should change any time you are a licensed foster parent, you will have to report this change to your agency.

- *Supervision*: Foster parents are responsible for the whereabouts, care, and supervision of a foster child at all times. If you, and your fellow foster parent, are employed outside the house, plans for your foster child's supervision must be determined prior to bringing a foster child into your home. Your child welfare agency will require prior approval for a child's supervision outside of your home, such as a day care environment.

Training: MAPP and PRIDE

After contacting the agency in your city, you will begin the first phase of your training, the pre-service portion. In some states, this is known as the Model Approach to Partnership in Parenting, or MAPP, while other states refer to this first training as Parent Resource for Information, Development, and Education, or PRIDE. Both of these initial training sessions concentrate on delivering information in regard to the basic requirements you will need if you choose to become a foster parent. As you begin this training, your state's child welfare agency will ask you to perform two important tasks: a criminal background history, and a home evaluation.

Criminal background checks are mandated by all states when becoming licensed to supervise and care for foster children in your home. Both your state's criminal justice service and the Federal Bureau of Investigation (FBI) will need to obtain a set of finger prints from you, as well as for each member of your household who is over the age of 18 years. Your finger prints will be kept on file by the agency. If an arrest or conviction should appear on your background check, you will be unable to be licensed as a foster parent.

Along with this background check, a home evaluation will also occur. During a home evaluation, your house will be inspected to determine if it is well maintained and clean enough for a foster child to stay in. Along with this, the child welfare agency will also determine if the house is properly heated and plumbing is in order; if there are adequate sleeping arrangements for each child; if smoke detectors are in place and working; and if all medication and cleaning equipment are safely stored away.

Each state has a different set of required hours of training. These required hours range from a minimum of four hours in states such as Illinois and Nevada, to 27 in Colorado, and a wide range in between. During your training sessions, the agency will help you to meet the needs, demands, and challenges that foster children face while under care. You will receive information and training on a wide range of topics. These include:

- Rights and responsibilities of a foster parent.

- Behavior management skills and the resources needed to best meet misbehavior.

- How to recognize abuse and neglect, and how to prevent them from happening.

- The social, personal, and family problems that often lead to a child being placed into foster care.

- Separation anxiety caused from being separated from one's family, and other issues dealing with a child's placement into foster care.

- Creating and expanding skills in showing love and attention to children who are disturbed and troubled.

- Gaining information about the stages of a child's development and abilities.

- Common health problems a foster child might face, and how to best address them.

- Understanding your own strengths and weaknesses, and how to use them effectively as a foster parent.

- How to work as a team with your caseworker, and other team work skills.

- Role and responsibilities of a caseworker.

- Relationship between foster parents, foster child, agency, and birth family.

- Understanding a birth parent's perspective of foster care.

- Reimbursement and the expenses involved.

Financially Supporting a Foster Child

Raising any child in today's society is financially challenging. Foster children are no different in that respect. Whether it is diapers and baby wipes, or clothes and high school graduation material, you are bound to spend money on your foster child. Your state's agency will reimburse you for much of it, though there may be times when you might spend your own money.

Your local agency will set the *per diem* rate, according to your foster child's age. A *per diem* rate is the daily amount of money you will receive in order to care properly for your child. Rates for children are broken down into three age groups: birth to 5, 6 to 12, and 13 to 18. The rate is furthermore separated into three other categories: basic, special, and exceptional. Basic payment is for those foster children who have not been identified for special or exceptional needs. Those children who have been tested for special or exceptional needs will receive a slightly higher rate of daily *per diem* reimbursement. In order for you, as a foster parent, to care for a special or exceptional child, you will be required to participate in additional training, as well as show that you are able to work with the professionals involved in the child's treatment plan.

When a foster child enters your house for the first time, you will receive an initial clothing allowance, again based on the child's age. In emergency situations, such as a child entering your home with only the clothes on his back, this initial allowance may be higher than normal. You will also have an annual clothing allowance, or amount that you may spend on clothing for your child for the calendar year. Any additional money spent that exceeds that amount may have to come out of your own personal account. All clothing purchased for your foster child belongs to him, and should be taken with him when he leaves your home and moves to another, or is reunited with his family. An additional allowance may be made for those items of clothing which fall into a special category, such as a school uniform or formal dress. Permission should be acquired from the caseworker before purchasing these items.

Diapers are a separate item, and may not fall under the clothing allowance, depending on the state's policy. Many states will allow you to buy diapers for children between the ages of birth to four years of age. These states will reimburse the full price of the diapers. Baby wipes are generally not included in this reimbursement.

As many foster parents have full-time jobs, child care is a necessity. Many agencies will reimburse the full price of child care for those foster parents who are employed full or part time. Some agencies may reimburse only a portion of the child care fee. You may also be reimbursed for school-related expenses, again according to your agency's policy. These expenses may include field trips, school club fees, books, graduation, and school pictures. School and summer camps may also be reimbursed if your agency permits it.

Additional Training

Each foster parent will be required to undertake ongoing training each year in order to keep the license up to date. The hours for this additional training will depend upon the agency's requirements. Training can be divided between the traditional format of in person and via a computer or video program. Many times, training hours and sessions are held through local foster parent association meetings. This additional training may focus on a number of topics, for example sexual abuse, CPR and first aid, discipline, cultural competency, behavior management, psychotropic medication, and working with birth parents.

Closing a Foster Home

The closing of a foster home generally occurs when foster parents feel they are no longer able to care for foster children in their homes. Once a home has been closed, the child welfare agency will no longer use it as a home for placement of foster children. If the foster parents of a closed home should wish to re-open their home for foster children again, the family and home will have to be re-evaluated by the child welfare agency in order to ensure that all criteria are met, and that the house passes inspection. There are also those occasions when the state may shut down a foster home, due to reasons of legality, illness, allegations, or other reasons they deem necessary. When this occurs, the foster child is removed from the home and placed into another.

In order to be a successful foster parent, it will take a great deal of training and preparation. The better prepared you are before your first foster child comes to live with you, the easier the transition will be, for both you and your foster child. With these tools, training, and resources at your disposal, you will now be ready to foster a child and help heal a broken heart.

CHAPTER 4

Placement

How to Prepare

Mike and Patty, foster parents of 20 years

When our family gets the "call" for a child coming into our home, we ask ourselves: are we ready and can we handle any issues that this child might be bringing to our home? Your life will change and you will deal with issues from your own kids. There will be jealousy a lot of times and there are also your kids' feelings that you have to address when a new child comes to your home.

When a new child arrives, we welcome them to the family, show them their rooms and try to treat them just as we might treat a relative coming for an extended visit. We have an extra room in our home that is for the new child; it has been painted many times and will probably be painted many more. Kids come into your home with many issues, which might include anger, and many will come with medication for ADHD, ADD, or mental issues and might peel paint off your walls, poke holes or other things that require you to redo a room; we just cover, patch and repaint. Then you get ready for the next one coming, thinking to yourself, "I wonder what this one will be like."

We try to keep a supply of diapers, wipes, and bottles on hand. We have a set of clothing in different sizes in the closet because you never know if the child will come with a lot of items or nothing but the clothes they have on. When the child arrives they might be scared, might be crying and are sometimes dirty. We introduce ourselves, we talk to the caseworkers and we try to just let the child relax and get used to being in our home.

I don't think you are ever really prepared for a new child coming into your home. When becoming a foster parent you are doing it because you truly love children.

The arrival of a new foster child in your house can be a time of excitement, as well as anxiety. The phone call from a caseworker asking if you would like a foster child placed in your home can leave you in a state of apprehension. It is often a time of questions, from you and your family, as well as from the foster child. For the child coming into your home, it is an especially intimidating period. Remember, this new foster child is being moved, against his wishes, to a strange home, and to an unknown family. While each child is unique, it is difficult to predict how each new foster child will react to this sudden and extreme change. Yet, with a little preparation and planning beforehand, you can ease the stress that is sure to occur in this transition.

In all areas of life, preparation beforehand is wise. Students in school have fire and tornado drills in order to be prepared for emergencies. Businesses often have first aid kits available if needed. Your household has probably prepared for emergencies, as well. You may have candles and flashlights in case you lose power. Perhaps you have extra food and water stored away. A fire extinguisher and fire alarm are probably located in your house in case of a disaster. Being prepared allows you to react better when a crisis or stressful situation should occur in your life. The placement of a new foster child in your life will certainly change your lifestyle and family environment in some way. Often, preparation beforehand is the key to a successful foster parent/child relationship.

Background Information

Perhaps the most important thing you can do to prepare for the arrival of a foster child is to educate yourself with as much background information and history as you can about the child. Do not be concerned if you have a large number of questions for your caseworker when you are first approached about the placement of a child in your house. While the caseworker may not have all the answers, you will find valuable information by asking. Some questions to consider include:

- How old is the child?

- Why is the child in care?

- How long might the child stay with you?

- Will the child need day care or supervision?

- Does the child have any learning disabilities or special needs of any kind?

- Does the child have any anger management or extreme emotional issues that you need to be aware of?

- Is this the first time the child has been in foster care?

- Are the child's medical shots up to date? Are there any medical concerns?

- Is the child from the same town? Does the child need to be enrolled in your local school system?

- Does the child have clothes? Will you need to buy diapers and baby wipes?

Family

The addition of a foster child to your household is sure to bring changes in your family dynamics. Many adjustments will have to be made in your home. After all, it is not just the adults in your house who will be fostering this child. Your own children will have an important role in the well-being and safety of your new arrival. Relatives may also be counted on to contribute to your foster child, as well. You may also find that neighbors, friends, and those you know from your place of worship, if you have one, will also wish to help you and your foster child.

Take some time to sit down with your children and remind them why you chose to be a foster parent. Share with them the information they need to know about your new foster child. If they are too young to understand why a child might be in foster care, do not burden or confuse them with this information; they will simply not need more information or details. Your older children may be curious as to why the foster child is coming to live with them. Share with them what you know, and remind them that the foster child is probably hurting, frightened, and may reject your family in the first few days and weeks. Tell your children that it will take time to form a relationship with the foster child. Your own children may have concerns. Perhaps they are worried that they will have to share you with their new foster sibling. They may resent that there is a new person joining their family. Ask them to share their feelings with you, and listen to what they have to say. Reassure your own children that you will always be there for them. You will also want to plan on setting aside some special time for just you and your own children, as they will need time alone with you during your fostering. Make sure you also set aside some special time for just you and your spouse. As a foster parent, you may become worn out and exhausted. If you do not give attention to your own marriage and your spouse, but instead focus only on being a parent to your children and your foster child, you may find your personal life suffering.

Getting your House Ready

Often, you want to have your house looking its best when company comes over. You probably do not want dirty dishes in the sink when your mother-in-law arrives. Spider webs in the ceiling are swept away before your annual Christmas party. When the boss comes over, you want your lounge room looking as clean as possible. You will want your home looking its best for your new arrival, too, as it helps to make him feel more comfortable and welcome in what is a very awkward and difficult transition.

Getting a house ready for a foster child is more extensive, though. You are responsible for providing a safe and healthy home environment for your child. Your home must be one that offers a feeling of security, as well as one that is welcoming to your new foster child. Having a checklist ready before your foster child arrives is important. Here is what you might have on your own checklist, depending on your foster child's age and needs:

- Alarm clock

- Baby crib and mattress

- Baby bottles

- Bed made with extra blanket if needed

- Car seat

- Closet space and extra hangers

- Diapers and baby wipes

- Dresser or cabinet for clothes

- Electrical outlets covered up

- Exposed wires taken care of

- Extra seat at kitchen table

- Fire extinguisher on every house floor/level

- Hair brush and comb

- Kitchen cleaning items out of reach

- Light fixtures working properly in all rooms, and nightlight in bedroom and nearby bathroom

- Medicines out of reach

- Mirror

- Soap, shampoo, conditioner, and toilet paper

- Toothpaste and toothbrush

- Towel

Welcoming your Child

The first impression you create with your foster child is often vitally important to how the next few days and weeks will transpire. This will probably not be the sweet little child who rushes into your waiting arms, laughing delightfully, as you might imagine. It is highly likely that your foster child will be scared and frightened, full of anxiety. He may have left his family moments ago, and is now told that you are his family, for the time being.

Without a doubt, he is full of questions, as emotions swirl within him. No matter how much this child has been abused, whether it is physically or emotionally, your foster child will want to have his mother and father back. After all, these people have been the most important people in his life. Along with this, he has lost his familiar pattern of living, his home, his friends, and all that made up his own personal world. Although it is impossible to predict how he will react when he first meets you, it is important that you approach this time with caution and care.

Each child's placement is different. Some may come to you with a head full of lice, while some might be covered in dirt, and the few possessions they own, if any, carried in a black plastic bag. In fact, they may only have the clothes on their back. Others may come to stay with you clean, healthy, and with a suitcase full of clothing, a box of possessions, and some money in their wallet. What is important is that you do not judge your foster child based on his arrival and appearance. However they arrive, they will need your patience, your time, and your love.

When the caseworker pulls into your driveway, if possible, go out to the car and welcome the caseworker and child, introducing yourself immediately, with a warm smile and soft voice. Inform your foster child who you are and the role you will now play in his life. He may very well not understand the foster care system, or what foster parents do. Do not insist that your new child call you mom or dad. In fact, it is wise that you never insist upon this. The word "mom" may refer to the person who beat him. "Dad" may be the person who left his family. Allow your foster child to call you by your first names, if you feel comfortable with this, or by whatever name he feels comfortable in calling you. As the child may be scared, do not insist that he react to you right away. This is a time of extreme difficulty, and your foster child may be in a state of shock. As you help him inside with his possessions, take him by the hand, if he is a little one, or place a soft hand upon his shoulder, if he is a teenager. Actions like these can be reassuring that all will be OK, that he is in a safe and caring home. Do not insist upon hugging, as he may be too embarrassed or hurt to do so.

After all introductions to the entire family have been made, take him on a tour of your house, his new home. Show him where he will sleep, and where his clothes will be kept. Have a nightlight already on in the room, if the room is dark. The smell of freshly baked chocolate chip cookies is always a welcome one in any home, particularly for children. Ask if he is hungry, and offer him some food. If he doesn't want any food, do not insist upon it. He will eat when he is ready and hungry.

You will have to sign some paperwork with your caseworker, as well as go over any last-minute news, details, and information. If possible, do this away from the child, as this, too, can be especially embarrassing and damaging to your new child. This is a good time for your foster child to eat, or be alone in his new room. If you have children of your own, it may also be a good time for them to engage in some sort of play with their new foster brother or sister. Your foster child is likely to be overwhelmed with the situation, so it is important that you make sure your home is as peaceful and quiet as possible. Do not invite the neighbors or relatives over upon arrival. Instead, allow your foster child to have some personal space and alone time. If it is late at night, do not insist that he go to bed immediately. After all, he is probably needing some time to reflect on the day's events, and sleep may be difficult to come by, as he is in a strange bed, in a strange home. Sadly, it is not uncommon for newly placed foster children to cry themselves to sleep during the first few nights. Do not be surprised if this happens. He may be scared and lonely. Let him know that you understand how difficult it is for him, and that his tears are normal and all right. Read him a bedtime story each night; place a nightlight not only in his room, but in the nearby bathroom, as well. Let him know that he can get up in the night and use the bathroom whenever he needs to.

Handling the First Few Days

As your foster child will need time to adjust to his new home and environment, he will require time and patience from you. To him, everything is new: new home, new food, new "parents," and "brothers and sisters," and new rules and expectations. Perhaps even a new school, along with students and teachers, as well, if he has moved from another school system. As a result, he may act out in a variety of ways. Your foster child may exhibit sudden outbursts of anger and aggressive behavior, extreme bouts of sadness and depression, or even imaginative stories about his birth family. He may even express no emotions at all. It is important that you do not take his behavior personally, as he attempts to understand his feelings, and cope the best way he can.

One of the difficulties that all encounter in the foster care system, whether it be foster parent, child, or caseworker, is the lack of information alongside the many questions that a placement brings with it. How long will the child remain in the foster home? When will the child see the parents next? How often can he visit with his family members? These are questions that will weigh heavy on your child's mind. Make sure you answer each question as honestly as you can. If you are unsure of an answer, let him know it, and reassure him that you will attempt to find out and let him know.

As soon as possible, take some time to sit down with your new foster child, and discuss the rules of your home, as well as your expectations of him. Listen to him, and encourage him to ask questions. This is an important time for your family, as you begin to form a relationship with your foster child. Spend time with him, and try to get to know him: his likes and dislikes, his fears and concerns, his hopes and dreams. If he wants, allow him to speak about his family. He may wish to brag about them to you. Do not judge his biological parents; instead, listen with an open ear and open heart, allowing him to see this, as it will encourage trust in you. Encourage him to put up pictures of his biological parents, birth family members, previous foster parents, and other important people in his life. Let him know that you understand how important these people are in his life.

All families have some sort of routine and patterns of behavior that exist within their home. Your own family may have a routine that you follow on a daily or regular basis. Depending upon the type of household your foster child came from, he may not be familiar with your day-to-day routine. Indeed, he may come from a home that had no set routine or schedule. He may have lived in a home where there were no expectations of him, and no rules for him to follow. It is important that you include your foster child in your family, and in your routine. Before expecting too much from him, give him some time alone to become comfortable with his new home, family, and surroundings. Allow him time to observe your family's routine before expecting him to participate actively. Some of your routines might be informal, such as dinner-time habits, shoes in the house, respect for others when speaking, and so on. If he has questions about your family's routine, answer them honestly, and at a level he can understand. Let him know why you do such activities in your house.

Time

The best gift you can give your foster child is the gift of time. He will need time to grieve the loss of his family; time to fully understand why he is in your home; time to learn your rules and expectations. He will need time to adjust to a new home, new family, and new school. He will also need time from you: time for someone to listen to him, to guide him, and time to instruct and teach him. It will also be very important for his mental well-being if you give him the time to laugh, to play, and most importantly, time to be cared for and loved.

As noted earlier, each time a foster child comes to live with you and your family, it will be a unique experience. Every placement will be different from each other, and it will not become routine. You are sure to have surprises from time to time, and some placements may even be unsettling. Preparation, a welcoming smile, and the gift of time will help your family and your foster child during this time of transition.

CHAPTER 5

Problems Foster Children Face

Tonya and Robert, foster parents of 12 years

Scotty and Brian arrived at our home one Tuesday after work. Scotty was four years old and his brother was five. They were both very small, and it looked like they had suffered from poor nourishment. If only that was what they suffered from. Both of them had been sold by their birth father for $500.00 in order to get some quick money. When the caseworker dropped them off, she warned us that the boys would suffer from behavioral problems.

Within the first five minutes of coming to our home, both of them were swearing like sailors. Ten minutes went by, and one of them wanted to urinate on the walls. They were highly strung, and were bouncing off the walls all night long. Unlike many foster children, they did not cry for their mother or father when the caseworker left, nor did they do it when they went to bed at night. In fact, they never once asked about going back home. The immediately called my husband and me "Daddy" and "Mommy;" they had serious attachment disorders, and had trouble forming those important bonds of healthy relationships with parental figures. Whatever these boys had seen and experienced in their short lives must have been very disturbing, very damaging, and very sad.

School was no easier. The school principal seemed to call us on a regular basis. One or both of the boys consistently got into severe trouble at school. Whether it was choking another student, hitting someone on the bus, or cursing at teachers, students, or the bus driver, both Scotty and Brian did not know how to behave properly. Even though their profanity was constant, and they were often abusive towards others, both boys seemed to be happy on the outside. They played well together, and both wore smiles on their faces on a regular basis.

Visitations were also disturbing. Oftentimes, the birth parents would not show up for the visits. Mother was nowhere to be found, and the father had made it clear to the caseworker that he did not want anything to do with his two sons. Instead, the boys would meet with grandparents. One visit saw the grandfather yelling and cursing at Brian for getting into trouble at school. It was no wonder to me that these boys were in the emotional and behavioral states they were. They had been surrounded by so much negativity, hostility, and rejection their whole young lives.

My husband and I have worked hard to show these boys as much love and compassion as we can. Scotty and Brian need someone to love them, and to love them unconditionally. They need guidance, and need to be taught how to behave in public and in the home. We have also been consistent in establishing and enforcing rules in our house. We feel that the boys need both love and structure the most, as these have been obviously lacking in their lives.

The placement of a child into your foster home is a life-changing experience for that foster child. Placement disruption is the term used when a child is removed from a home and placed into the custody of a child welfare agency, and thus into a foster home. For many, it is a frightening time, as the fear of the unknown can quickly overwhelm a child. Others are filled with anger, as they emotionally reject the idea of being separated from their family members. Feelings of guilt may also arise within the foster child, as the child may believe that he or she may have had something to do with the separation from the birth family. Some children experience self-doubt, as they feel that they simply did not deserve to stay with their family. For all, it is a traumatic experience that will forever alter the lives of foster children.

Many psychologists state that it is necessary for young children to form a relationship with at least one main parental figure or caregiver in order for the child to develop socially and emotionally. As the child will have formed some sort of relationship with his parent, the removal of a child from his home and placement into another's home through foster care, is often a difficult, traumatic experience. Often, the removal of a child from home occurs after a caseworker has gathered evidence and presented this evidence to a court, along with the recommendation that the child be removed. Indeed, most foster care placements are made through the court system.

As distressing as this may be for a child, it will be even more traumatic if the removal from the child's birth home comes without any notification. These emergency removals often occur late in the evening. As caseworkers remove a child from home suddenly, most are unprepared. Foster children leave their home with a quick goodbye, leaving behind most of their belongings, with a few clothes and perhaps a prized possession hurriedly stuffed into a plastic bag. Before they know it, they are standing in front of you, strangers, people they have never met before. Against their will, they are in a strange home, their new home. For most, it is a time of fear, a time of uncertainty, a time when even the bravest of children become scared.

Many times, children placed into foster care suffer from mental health issues. A placement disruption may be so severe that the child feels as if their entire world is falling apart. For them, it is. Everything they know to be true in their world is now turned upside down. The family they lived with, grew up with, laughed with, and cried with is no longer there to take care of them. The bed they woke up in each morning is now different. For too many foster children, the school they went to, the teachers they learned from, and the friends they had formed relationship with, have also been taken from them. Instead, these children now live with a strange family, wake each morning in a different house, sit in an unfamiliar classroom, and are no longer surrounded by those who love and know them best. Children in foster care often struggle to deal with and survive these traumatic events, as they struggle to adjust to a new home and new family.

Anxiety Disorders

Issues from anxiety can manifest themselves in a number of ways. Perhaps the one that foster children face the most is separation anxiety, an excessive concern that children struggle with concerning the separation from their home, family, and from those they are attached to the most. Indeed, the more a child is moved, from home to home, from foster placement to another foster placement, or multiple displacements, the bigger the concern becomes. Those children who undergo multiple displacements often create walls to separate themselves in an attempt to not let others into their lives. In attempting to do so, many foster children end up lying to their foster families, as they try to keep their new family at a distance, and at the same time, give themselves a sense of personal control.

Other anxiety disorders include *obsessive-compulsive disorder*, where a child repeats unwanted thoughts, actions, and/or behavior out of a feeling of need. *Panic disorders* find a child experiencing intense bouts of fear for reasons that may not be apparent. These attacks may be sudden, and unexpected, as well as repetitive in their nature. Panic disorders also may coincide with strong physical symptoms, such as shortness of breath, dizziness, throbbing heartbeats, or chest pains. Another anxiety disorder that foster children may face is *social phobias*, or the fear of being embarrassed or facing the criticism of others.

Depression Disorders

The loss of a family may result in a foster child spiraling into depression. These feelings of depression may intrude into all areas of a foster child's life, from their capability to act and function in the home to their school environment and the interaction with those their own age. Children who suffer from a depressive disorder may show strong and continuous signs of sadness. They may also have great difficulty in focusing on school work or life around them, and may instead concentrate on death or suicidal feelings. Loss of appetite or severe changes in eating habits may also be a result of a depressive disorder. Feelings of guilt over the placement may also overwhelm a foster child. Finally, a child who suffers from a depressive disorder may lack energy in day-to-day tasks, or may have difficulty sleeping.

Anger

Dealing with separation and loss is difficult for anybody. As an adult, you have had experience with this, and know who and where to reach out to when in need of help. Foster children, though, generally do not know how to handle these feelings and emotions. Yet, these feelings must be released, in some fashion. One way of expressing feelings of isolation is to lash out in anger and frustration to those around them. Though foster children do not necessarily blame you, the foster parent, or the caseworker, the feelings of frustration and loss are strong within them, and you may be the only one they can release them to. Anger may also result in destruction of property or items within your foster home, as the child lashes out.

Mental Health

In regard to the mental health of a foster child, placement disruptions in a foster child's life increase the chances that the child will be at greater risk of experiencing future mental health services. The longer a foster child stays within the same foster home, the greater chance of emotional bonding, and thus a sense of stability is formed, which is beneficial in regard to social behavior, and academic performance in school, in the community, as well as in your foster home.

To be sure, there are high levels of mental health problems with children under foster care. The majority of foster children face the reality that most of their mental health problems are not being addressed as needed. Furthermore, psychological and emotional issues that challenge foster children may even worsen and increase, rather than improve and decrease, while under placement in foster homes and care. Foster children, in many cases, do not receive adequate services in regard to mental health and developmental issues and are not likely to do so in the near future, due to lack of government funding and lack of resources, as well as the simple matter that child welfare caseworkers are understaffed and overworked, in most states across the country.

School Performance and Misbehavior

Foster children often have a difficult time with exhibiting proper school behavior during the school day. For many of the children, school is a constant reminder that they are, indeed, foster children without a true home. Their peers are living with biological family members while they are not. This can be a difficult reality for them, and can be manifested in several ways, such as displaying aggressive behavior, disruptive behavior, defiance, and low self-esteem. Some foster children simply withdraw and become antisocial, in an attempt to escape the current environment into which they have been thrust. For many foster children, violent behavior becomes the norm, as they act out in a negative and disruptive fashion not only in the school, but also in their foster home. This can prompt another move to another foster home and another school.

As a result of this behavior, foster children often face greater risks of suspension from school, affecting their academic standing. They may repeat a grade level, or may simply be placed in classes that are not appropriate to their age level. Those children who suffer from depression have a much higher rate of behavior disorders, including violent behavior, which often results in school suspension. Foster children and the challenges they face while in school will be discussed in greater depth in Chapter 8.

Aging Out: Leaving Foster Care

Being placed in a foster home is bad enough for a foster child. Sadly, for far too many foster children, leaving the foster care system is even more traumatic. As a foster child reaches the age of 18, in most states in the United States, and in many other countries, the child "ages out" of the foster system, and begins the transition into "the real world."

Eighteen is a difficult age for any teenager. Sure, it is a time of independence, freedom, and change; at least it is in the eyes of many when they reach that magic age. It is a time of moving out of a home, finding a job, joining the military, and going off to college. Typically, children from traditional homes have parents who are able to guide them through these changes, providing help and advice as these 18-year-olds determine the next stage in their lives. Along with this, most young adults are still able to rely on their parents not only for good advice, but also for financial help. Foster children, though, do not have these resources, these lifelines so to speak, to help out as they try to ease into their own lives of independence. When they are sick, there is no one to take care of them. Struggling in college? Often, there is no one to help them with their studies. Car broken down? Most former foster children have no one to turn to for help.

Foster children who age out of care often leave the foster system without the necessary skills, experiences, or knowledge they need in order to adjust well to society. Without a family to turn to once they age out, many foster children find themselves in difficult times and situations. These young adults, who are involuntarily separated from their foster families through the intervention of the government, face higher rates of homelessness, as most have no options for future housing. Unemployment in the United States is higher among former foster children than among other young people, and many struggle financially (Courtney *et al.* 2005). This may be due to the fact that roughly 50 percent of those foster children who age out do not complete high school. Even more disturbing is that these young people are more than twice as likely not to have a high school diploma than others their own age. Less than 30 percent of former foster children ever make it to college, let alone graduate with a degree. Similar conditions exist in Australia and Europe, as well (Mendes and Moslehuddin 2006; O'Higgins 2001; Stein 2006).

Proper health care also remains a problem for former foster children. While under the care of a child welfare system, foster children in the United States do in fact receive free health care through Medicaid. Medical treatment and essential medicine are part of the right of each foster child, while under care. Yet, when a child ages out, this health care is no longer provided, leaving many without any type of insurance or care. Along with this, access to mental health and additional support organizations is also difficult to come by. Accordingly, countless former foster children have untreated mental health needs, as well. Aged-out female foster children also have higher pregnancy rates than females their own age from traditional homes; nearly 50 percent of young women were pregnant inside of a year to 18 months after leaving the foster care system (Sullivan 2009). It comes as no surprise that many former foster children end up in some sort of incarceration.

Helping your Foster Child through Positive Relationships

Your foster child needs your help, your support, and most importantly, your unconditional love. As many of these children are coming from homes and environments where they have experienced abuse and neglect, as well as a host of other problems, they may be resistant to your help, and to your love. Do not be discouraged, as this is quite normal with foster children. Remember, they have been taken from their homes and their families, and are now living with strangers. No matter how poorly they have been treated, no matter how much abuse they have suffered, they still want to be with their family members, as it may be the only love they have experienced.

As mentioned in the last chapter, the first few hours and days with a foster child are often the most difficult days you will experience as a foster parent. Your biggest weapon to combat the challenges you and your foster child face is consistency. If you are consistent in your love, your support, and your help, you will begin to tear through those walls your foster child has erected, and begin the much-needed healing process for your foster child. The setting of rules and expectations are of the utmost importance in the first few days, and we shall look at those in full in the next chapter. Just as important for your foster child, as it is for all children, is the foundation of a positive and nurturing relationship between you and your foster child. Without this, your job as a foster parent will be all the more difficult.

Trust and Compassion

When a child is suddenly taken from his home, and from his family, and placed in a home against his will, there are bound to be issues of trust. One way to combat this is to create a trusting and nurturing environment within your own home. Let your foster child know as early as possible that he is welcome in your house. Along with this, you will want to let your foster child know that your house is a safe one, and that he will not come to harm in your home. Not only do you want to let your foster child know this when he joins your family, it is just as important to remind him of this as often as possible. You want to show your foster child that you value him as a person, and that he is important. What he says, what he thinks, what he believes: your foster child needs to realize that all of these are important. For some children, this might be a new experience, as they have never been shown that they are valued before.

Trust can also be built by showing your foster child that you care for him. Building a trusting relationship means showing your foster child that you are concerned for his well-being, physically, emotionally, and mentally. Showing compassion for your foster child is an important part of building a healthy relationship, as he needs to know and feel that you care for him. After all, close relationships between children and adults is a central part of avoiding further risky behavior. Trust, though, does take time, and for some foster children, it may take a very long period of time. Remember, you are planting seeds, here, that you may never see come to fruition.

Empathy

Many of the situations and environments your foster child left before coming to live with you are distressing, troubling, and even heartbreaking. As a foster parent, you will be able to build a stronger relationship with your foster child by trying to understand their feelings from their perspective. By doing so, not only do you better appreciate their feelings and emotions, but also why they may act a certain way, behave in a particular manner, and say the things they do. Empathy also helps in breaking down the walls between you and the child, as your compassion and love for the child grows.

Encourage Good Behavior

Like all children, your foster child wants to feel like he not only belongs to your family, but also that he plays an important role in your household. If your foster child does not believe that he contributes in a meaningful way in your home, he may seek someplace else to do so. This "someplace else" may not be a place which you want your child to be associated with. Thus, it is vital that you encourage good behavior in your home.

Find your foster child doing something well, and notice him for it. Tell him that you appreciate what he has done, thanking him for it. This can be as simple as cleaning up a room, taking the garbage out, playing quietly in a room, completing homework, hanging up a bath towel, or a number of small details that normally may go unnoticed. No matter how small the action is, it is essential to your foster child's well-being that he feels recognized and that his actions are significant.

When a child is acknowledged for a behavior or action, no matter if it is negative or positive, he will more often than not repeat that same action. Therefore, it is necessary as a foster parent to recognize quickly the positive ones and focus upon those, however brief. Good behavior deserves recognition, in all areas of life. As an adult, you appreciate when someone recognizes the work you do, whether it is at your work, in your place of worship, if you have one, or in your house. You, too, enjoy it when someone notices all the hard work you put in. It makes you feel good. Your foster child needs this positive encouragement even more than you do. After all, the self-esteem of your foster child is most likely to be at an extremely low point. It is part of your role as a foster parent to bring a sense of self-worth back to your foster child.

Listen

Your foster child more than likely has gone through a great deal of trauma. Feelings and emotions are swirling up inside him, and your child will need an outlet. Simply putting all else aside for a time, sitting down, and listening, will help your foster child develop a better sense of self-worth, as you validate his thoughts, feelings, and emotions. As your foster child has had many experiences outside your own home, it is important to remember not to judge him, or be critical as you listen. Simply let him talk, while you listen. If your foster child brings up something that the caseworker needs to know, then it is your responsibility to inform the caseworker.

Quality Time

Nothing says you care for a child more than spending quality time with that child. Spending time with your foster child and focusing on him is important for the mental health of the child. Including your foster child in family activities is essential for the well-being of your household. These might include going to the movies, parks, church, or other faith-based activities as a family. If your foster child is interested in joining a local sports team, like a recreational or school baseball team, then encourage the child to try it out, and attend the games he plays in. Learn what hobbies your foster child enjoys, and join in with them. Invite him to help you make dinner, and eat as a family together. Above all, be excited and enthusiastic about your foster child and what his interests are.

Your foster child will no doubt come to you with a myriad of problems. Whether these problems be emotional, psychological, or physical, the problems will be too difficult for him to overcome by himself. He will need your love, support, kindness, patience, and compassion. With the proper training and knowledge, never doubt that you will make a difference in the life of your foster child.

CHAPTER 6

Creating Rules and Expectations

Shannon and Jim, foster parents of 12 years

A winter storm watch is issued and lots of things must be done in the next day or two to prepare. The weather forecast is for ice, snow, and extremely cold temperatures and it will last two to four days at least. So, our family of six has begun preparations and then...the phone rings. The child welfare agency is calling and they need a placement for a sibling group of three. After finding out a bit (and I mean a tiny bit) about the children and discussing it with our family, we agree to take the children in to our home. These children, ages three, four, and 11, have been traveling across the country and have now been located and will be returning home by airplane. The plane is scheduled to land tonight, plenty of time (about 24 hours) to get them settled and buy them the necessities. The phone rings again; the four-year-old is having trouble breathing and they are headed to the hospital. They should be able to catch a plane in the morning and will arrive the next evening. Now we are looking at hours before the storm; I am a bit nervous. When the plane arrives, we arrange to meet one of the child welfare agency workers at Wal-Mart so we can get the kids some essentials and make it home before the storm which is just hours away. Now that everyone is settled, and we are all home safe, the work begins.

The children arrive with a variety of sickness, the flu, asthma, pinworms, and scabies. The storm hits and the four-year-old is up all night coughing, wheezing, and throwing up. We are heartbroken for these children and know only a fraction of what they have been through in their lifetime. I cannot imagine what they have been through in the last couple of weeks, but one thing is certain...it is our job to create a safe environment, set expectations, and explain the rules.

Creating a safe environment sounds like a logical, obvious first step and it also sounds like the easiest. A safe environment doesn't just consist of a warm bed, food to eat, and locks on the doors. A safe environment for these children takes a lot of work and time on the part of the foster family. We have to constantly reinforce with words that we will not harm them in any way; we will provide them with meals every day and also snacks if they are hungry. Many of these children have experienced extreme hunger so having food is a huge concern for them. Rules and expectations are also very important. Many of these children haven't had any consistency so they are looking for boundaries. These boundaries must be explained and discussed. The expectations and rules must be the same for everyone, both biological children and foster children. This is so important to the dynamics of your "new family." Discussing expectations, rules, and consequences seems like a lot to overwhelm the children with, but it is essential to the family as a whole. Simple things that are important in your household may be unheard of to the children entering your homes. Some children have never been taught "manners." Some children do not know how to bathe, or dry off with a towel before they get dressed. Some children may not know how to eat with a fork or sit at a dinner table. Turning lights off when you leave a room or taking your shoes off before you enter the house are probably things that they have never done, so please be patient and reinforce the small things with positive encouragement. They will learn and life does get easier. The kids really do like structure, and they will rise to the top when your expectations are high but attainable.

The moment a foster child comes to live with you, his whole world has changed. There are now different rules and different expectations to follow for him. Your house is a new environment for him. There is even a set of new parents for him. Everything he has known to be true is now different. These are significant changes in the child's lifestyle. All decision making has been taken away from him. The child is in your house against his own will, against his own choice.

There is a good chance that any rules and expectations you have for your foster child will not be met. This is especially true in the first few days and weeks. This is a time to gain trust as well as simply get to know each other. It may take a while, but as a foster parent, you are in it for the long, tough haul. Make no mistake, it is often tough. For many foster children, they have been given up on numerous times. You just might be the first adults in their lives who will not give up on them. They may resist you, and may resist all that you have to offer. This is normal for foster children. Remember, they may very well not want to be in your home, as it is not their own home. They may not want to be living with your family when they come to you, as it is not their own family. You could be the bad guy in this situation, and you can't expect them to embrace you and your family immediately, or even to like you.

As discussed in the last chapter, it is essential that you build a positive relationship with your foster child. This will help to ease the transition, as well as contribute to the mental well-being of your foster child, and to the dynamics of your own household. What is also important to remember is that foster children need structure, guidance, and consistency, in all areas. This includes the setting of rules and expectations in your household. In order for your household to run smoothly, you must set some rules in place, and let your foster children know what expectations you have of them.

Perhaps the most important element to setting rules and expectations, though, is to remember where your foster child came from. He may never have had rules of any kind in his home. Your foster child may not have had the responsibility of doing chores. Homework may be something completely foreign to him, as it may not have been expected or enforced. Manners may not have been taught or modeled in his family. Even personal hygiene may not have been established before he came to live with you.

With this in mind, it is important to set up some rules and expectations, though, early on with your foster child. As expectations and rules may make or break your foster child, you need to be realistic with your expectations from the child. You also need to ensure that your family's values and moral structure do not change. You probably do not accept violent behavior, disrespectful attitudes, profanity, or destruction of property within your home. Yet, many foster children have not been brought up in this manner, and you may find that your foster child does not understand your values and morals. One of your biggest challenges as a foster parent will be to remain patient with your foster child's progress as you teach him the kind of behavior you expect from him in your home, and not insist upon it all at once. If you do demand the type of behavior that you expect from your own family, you may push your foster child even further away. Work on the behaviors first that you find most important. When your foster child has improved with one expectation, then it is time to begin focusing on another. All children enjoy praise from the adults in their lives. Sadly, your foster child may never have received praise before, nor had the opportunity to be successful in a given task.

When you feel the time is ready, sit down with your foster child and let him know of your expectations. Be very specific, yet simple at the same time, in your explanation of your rules and expectations, ensuring that your foster child understands what you would like him to do, and how he should behave. Make sure that they are appropriate for his age, as well as ability level. These expectations must be reasonable, as he might not be able to handle too much, due to his previous living environment. Do not expect perfection, as his abilities might be quite low. There will be times he will resist, or not perform as you would like. This is fairly normal, and probable. Instead, look for opportunities to praise your foster child when he does something positive.

When establishing rules in your household with your foster child, it is important that you continue to stick to the rules you already have established. Foster children will shake up your household like nothing else. Therefore, continuing to adhere to the rules that you normally have will keep consistency with your family members. Speaking of consistency, it is vital that you are consistent with your rules. Children need consistency in all areas of their life, and foster children especially so. They may test you, and seek to see if you are consistent. After all, they may have lived in a home where there was no consistency in any aspect of their life. Besides your own set of house rules, foster children need some basic rules in order to grow in their health and well-being, as well as to keep them safe and free from harm.

Supervision

Children always need supervision, and your foster child is no different in that aspect. You need to know where your foster child is at all times. Where is your foster child when school is over? Who is taking your foster child to day care? What is your foster child involved in outside of your home? Who are the adults in charge when your foster child is not in your presence? Is the child in a safe environment? Is the child in a positive environment? These are all questions that you need to focus upon as a foster parent, as it will help to ensure that your foster child is in the most productive and safest environment possible, and out of danger.

As a foster parent, you have the responsibility of knowing your foster child's whereabouts at all times. If your foster child should wish to spend the night at a friend's house, you must have prior approval from the caseworker, as criminal history and police background checks must be made. If your child is in day care while you are at work, the day care must be approved by the caseworker, as well. If your foster child should be involved in after-school activities, you are responsible for meeting the supervising adult in charge, as well as ensuring that there will be adult supervision at all times. In the United States, some states do not approve of teenagers babysitting foster children, while some states go even further and state that no adult may do so either, unless this has been approved by the caseworker, and a criminal history has been verified. Finally, if your family decides to travel out of state for travel or vacation, you must also gain prior caseworker approval.

Friends and Family

Before your foster child was placed in your home, he may have developed strong relationships with others. Perhaps these were friends his own age, or members of his family or family's circle of friends. These relationships will have a strong influence on your child, both in a positive and negative fashion. It will be most important, whenever possible, to meet your foster child's friends, and parents, and try not only to establish rules, but also attempt to determine if the friend will have a positive or negative influence. While you may have to discourage your foster child from going to a friend's house, or not permit it, you should still encourage him to invite his friends to your house, and create a welcoming atmosphere in your home. It is much easier to supervise your foster child while he is under your own roof. Your foster child, though, may have a difficult time making new friends, due to the amount of times he has been moved from one home to another. Along with this, he may be hesitant to let others know that he is in foster care, and may not be open to you meeting these friends. Let him know, though, that he must have permission from you before inviting anyone over.

Your foster child will, more than likely, visit with his birth family from time to time. It is not uncommon for a foster child to let his birth parents know about your rules, especially if the child disagrees with your rules and expectations. In hopes of testing your parental limits, he may encourage his birth parents to speak up on his behalf. Some birth parents have been known to oppose the rules you have set in place. If you have the opportunity, it may be helpful if you meet with the birth family and discuss why you have certain rules and expectations in place. Reassure them that you have not only the safety of their child in mind, but also his best interests, as well. This will demonstrate that you care about their child, as well as respect their concerns.

Television and Music

Music has always been a part of a teenager's lifestyle. From the days of Elvis and The Beatles to today's top musicians, teens have helped catapult singers to the top of the charts. Yet, today's musicians are a little bit different than Elvis and The Beatles. Gone are the days when "I Wanna Hold Your Hand" was causing parents to shout in protest, fearing their child was being exposed to harmful lyrics. Many of today's musicians suggest a lot more than "holding someone's hand," or heading over to "Heartbreak Hotel." Music in the early twenty-first century leaves little to the imagination for young teens, while some even espouse violence towards those in authority. For parents, the music field can be a dangerous minefield to maneuver through.

Even more challenging for parents is the television set. "Leave it to Beaver" and "The Brady Bunch" are ancient history and are not shows that foster children recognize. Instead, television is a place where children can be exposed to nudity, profanity, and violence, on a grand scale. With the advent of cable and satellite television, there is an endless supply of harmful shows for children.

This is not to say that all television is harmful. Indeed, in moderation, television can be beneficial. Small children can get a head start in school by learning simple alphabetical and counting skills on children's programs. Older children can learn facts about history, geography, politics, and other information by viewing educational programs. But, like anything in life, too much of a good thing can be dangerous. Children who watch more than four hours a day, on a consistent basis, tend to be overweight. Those children who watch programs that show acts of violence carried out tend to display their own violent tendencies. As a result, many children become desensitized to violence and violent behavior (Mayo Clinic 2011). Along with this, children who are subject to violence on television also may become frightened by the world around them, as they feel the world they live in is simply a reflection of what they see on television.

Drug and alcohol abuse, cigarettes, and other forms of risky and dangerous behavior also run rampant on some television programs. Often, drug usage and premarital sex are glorified on television, and displayed as being exciting and acceptable. Unfortunately, these acts are not necessarily shown on just the television programs themselves. Commercials also expose children to these types of behavior (Federal Trade Commission 2007). Children watch up to 25,600 commercials each year, on average. While many commercials market themselves to children, just as many marketers use commercials to advertise towards a more adult market. Constant exposure to commercials does affect a child, whether on a conscious or subconscious level.

There are a number of strategies you can use, as a foster parent, when supervising your foster child's television viewing habits:

- Set a good example with your own viewing habits. Your child is watching you watch television.

- Make sure you limit the amount of time your child watches television each day, and each week, and encourage your foster child to find other alternatives for entertainment.

- Make sure the television is turned off while you sit down to eat, preferably as a family together, and ensure that your foster child is not distracted with his homework with the television on in the background. In fact, there is no reason why your foster child should have a television in his room. No matter how much he asks or pleads, keep the television out of his bedroom.

- Preview what your child watches beforehand. If he enjoys watching a favorite program every day, or every week, find out what it is, and watch it to determine if it is appropriate for him.

- Look for shows that your entire household can watch, and invite your foster child to sit down with you and spend some family time together.

- Make sure that all homework and after-school chores are attended to first before the television goes on. Perhaps a ban on all television during the weekdays is necessary.

- Talk to other parents, foster parents, friends, and teachers about their television habits and rules, and find out what shows they recommend.

- Most importantly, let your foster child know what your own beliefs are in regard to what is on the television, and discuss with them what they are watching.

Technology

The internet! For many foster parents, it can be a whole new world. It can be a wonderful world for your child. The internet has become a global tool, and a valuable resource. Children today rely on the internet for a variety of reasons, including education. There is a tremendous number of educational websites for you to use when helping your foster child with their school work. Whether it is math, social studies, science, English, or even music and the arts, you can find all the help you need on the internet.

Cell phones, smartphones, and other mobile phone devices are also wonderful technological tools that your children have come to depend on as a major part of their lives. As a foster parent, these phones can help you keep track of your foster child, as well as allow your child's caseworker to keep in constant contact with the child. These devices also will allow you to monitor your foster child's activities, as these devices permit you to view who the child has been in previous contact with, as well as determine what websites your child has been looking at.

Yet, just like the radio and television, there are also hazards, as well. More than one out of every ten teenagers has posted a naked picture of themselves online (Lenhart 2009). Not only is this dangerous in the present, a "digital tattoo" (digital identity) can haunt them for the rest of their lives. This is only one of the dangers of spending time on social network sites, such as Twitter and Facebook, and using blogs and texting. It can be a playground with no parental supervision. It is easy for children to access inappropriate content while on the internet. Many times, users are introduced to this content against their wishes, as the content can suddenly appear without warning, either through pop-up screens, or through mistakenly typing in a wrong website address.

Cyber bullying has become a frightening reality for today's youth. Hurtful and derisive comments and taunts by bullies while on the playground and within a school can be harmful enough but cyber bullying can be even more damaging to a child. This form of bullying occurs when threats, insults, gossip, and negative comments about a child are spread online through social networks, emails, and instant messaging or texting. When cyber bullying is posted on a social network, it can quickly spread throughout a community, and into the cyber world.

Sexting is the act of sending a naked picture or a sexually inappropriate message to someone else. Twenty percent of children today have reported receiving a sext message (Sherman 2009). The same study shows that children as young as nine years of age reported having been introduced to sext messages.

Online predators are often a parent's worst technological nightmare. Usually posing as young people, predators attempt to befriend children and form close relationships through the use of the internet. Predators will often gather personal information about the child in an attempt to lure the child away from his home for their own purposes, often ending in tragic results.

Foster parents need to be concerned for the safety and privacy of their foster child with social networking. Help your child understand this, remind him of the dangers of posting, know how he is getting online, put privacy settings in place, and know what your foster child is posting. In order to keep your foster child safe, you may also consider:

- Setting time limits for when your foster child may use a cell phone or iPod Touch.

- Talking about internet safety with your foster child.

- Taking advantage of parental controls available through most cell phone carriers.

- Charging the phone/device in your room, or in a place where you can monitor the phone's use during evening hours.

- Taking your foster child's phone or smartphone each night and checking the text messages both received and sent.

- Keeping home computers in a common area of the house, not in your foster child's room, where you can monitor use.

- If you allow your foster child to have an email account or social network site, such as Facebook, make sure you have the password as well as being a "friend" on the social network page, so you can edit any harmful content posted.

- Reminding your foster child that words DO hurt, and that they should not say anything in texts, emails, or social pages that they wouldn't say face to face.

- Reminding your foster child that what they post online, whether it is words or pictures, can impact their future schools, careers, and scholarships.

Drugs and Alcohol

If you are fostering a teen in your home, chances are that he may have experimented with drugs or alcohol. He may have also picked up the habit of smoking. As a foster parent, you cannot allow these in your home. Therefore, you must be clear that these are not permitted. There should be no smoking at any time in the home, or while he is away from home. Let him know that he is not to have possession of matches, lighter, or any other form of tobacco or drug material at any time. Let him know what the consequences will be beforehand. If he has already experimented with these prior to coming to your home, he might very well resist you strongly in this, setting up confrontational moments between him and your family. Be prepared for this, and remain consistent.

Children are in need of boundaries and rules. In fact, all children like to know beforehand what is to be expected of them, and what they can and cannot do. One of the most important life lessons you can teach your foster child is the lesson of rules and consequences. By taking time in the beginning to establish rules and expectations with him, you will help to make his stay with you a more pleasant one: one that he will most certainly grow and learn from, as well.

CHAPTER 7

Your Foster Child and His Development

Sheryl and William, foster parents of 23 years

Little Michael was only five years old when he came to live with us. It was easy to see, from the first day, that Michael had some learning disabilities. Michael's speech was almost non-existent. He could speak no more than two or three words at a time. Michael also had a tough time trying to understand simple directions. It was difficult for all of us during the first few weeks, as we tried to get to know Michael, as well as for him as he tried to adjust to our house rules and our family.

When Michael came to us, there was very little information about his development stage and any learning disabilities. His caseworker had not been made aware of any by his birth family, so there was nothing to share with us. As he had not spent much time in school, due to his young age, there was no information from his previous school to help us as we tried to help Michael.

My husband and I quickly learned that we had to be an advocate for little Michael in school. In order to get him the help he needed, Michael needed to be in a class that could best address his learning disabilities. This was a problem, though, as our young foster child had not been tested for such a class. As he was new to the school, we found out that he was not at the top of the list to be tested. So, I had to fight for my little foster son.

Emails, phone calls, and even visits to the school: these were all steps I had to take in order to get Michael the resources he needed. I had to make a bit of a pest of myself, but it worked out to Michael's advantage. After a month and a half, Michael was finally able to get into the class he needed, and have the special attention that his learning disability required.

My husband and I worked with him for the five months he was with us. Sadly, we made very little progress with his speech. We also worked on sight words [his weekly spelling words/words frequently used and repeated in his books] for his class, but Michael never really picked up on them. He might learn a word or two here and there each evening, but would not recall them the next night when we went over them again. By the end of the five months, it seemed we were no further ahead with our little foster child than when he came to our home.

When Michael moved back to his biological parent's house, he was moved out of our school system and returned to his old one. I found out later that Michael was not receiving any additional help with his learning disability, as he had not been tested at the school he was enrolled in.

We have had other foster children come into our home. Many of them have had some sort of developmental challenge. Some have had emotional disorders, many have had social disorders. Yet, little Michael's learning disabilities affected him in a big way. He simply could not communicate with us, or anyone. We only hope that we planted a little seed in him that will soon open up and bloom.

The normal development of a child can often pose some difficult times for even the most patient of parents. As a child moves through different stages of his life, each stage comes with its own set of developmental tasks. Foster children, though, may have this normal development disrupted, due to the significant and specific challenges they face from their background. As a foster parent, you will be better equipped to help your foster child if you not only understand the normal development of a child, but also some of the risks and potential problems associated with foster children, as they age from birth to 18 years of age.

Certainly, every child is a unique person, and thus will develop differently than the next, with children developing at different speeds and at different rates. Generally, though, there are four main categories that each child will experience in his development. These include the cognitive, emotional, physical, and social categories:

- *Cognitive*: As a child grows in age, he will experience growth intellectually. His language will increase in terms of vocabulary development, as he first learns to speak and recite the alphabet, and he will eventually gain a larger personal vocabulary, conversational ability, and writing skills.

- *Emotional*: Trust is vital for a child. In order for a child to progress normally, he must learn to trust not only those who care for him, but also the environment around him. He must be able to recognize what is safe, as well as what might be harmful to him. His caregivers must be trusting, loving individuals who will teach him how to properly recognize and express his own feelings and emotions.

- *Physical*: As a child grows in size, their ability to crawl, walk, run, and jump (gross motor skills) will also increase. Along with this, their ability to work with their hands, doing activities such as writing, cutting with scissors, and holding dinner utensils (fine motor skills) will increase, as well.

- *Social*: The development of social skills is necessary in order for a child to successfully interact with his peers, as well as form healthy relationships with others. It is also important that the child develop the ability to empathize with others, thus understanding the needs of others and reacting to them in a positive and socially acceptable manner.

Ages of Development

Generally, a child will develop certain skills and abilities as he ages. It is important to remember that what may be normal for one child can be different for another. Children placed in foster care often exhibit significant behavior problems as compared to those children who come from traditional homes. Those children who have experienced abuse, neglect, or trauma in their lives are more likely to be delayed in development, or may even regress to a younger stage, due to the stress they suffer from. Many foster children also suffer from internalizing their concerns and fears, causing additional harm as a result. Foster children are also more likely to fall further behind in their development while under foster care supervision. In order to better help your foster child, it is essential that you become familiar with his development. A list of what to expect for each stage of normal development, as well as what you might expect from a foster child at each particular age category both follow. Also included are some guidelines and suggestions to consider as you try to assist your foster child through each age group development.

Baby: 0–12 months

- Develops own pattern of feeding and sleeping
- Brain is developing through use of senses
- Sleeps a great deal
- Swift growth
- Motor skills begin to develop
- Strong attachment to mother figure
- Begins to vocalize
- Enjoys repeating tasks over and over
- Loves to be held and hugged
- Requires a great deal of love, affection, and nurturing
- Plays by himself

Development in this stage of life is one of the first steps at building loving and trusting relationships. If a baby should suffer from neglect or abuse during this formative time, the effects can last a lifetime. Foster parents often believe that they can effectively "heal" the child from his abuse. The truth is, the effects from neglect and abuse may need a lifetime of healing, and may require a great deal of both medical and psychological attention. When taking a foster baby who suffers from abuse or neglect into your home, it is best that you surround yourself with as much information and support as you possibly can. You simply will not be able to help "heal" the child by yourself. You can, though, provide a healing and nurturing environment for him, one that will help him in his early stages of life.

Foster babies suffering from abuse may show a number of symptoms. He may have a hard time getting to sleep, or waking up. His body may be wracked with movement during his sleep, as it is a fretful one. Some babies suffer from delays in motor skills, as well as in speech. Another result of trauma may result in a baby who is quiet and non-responsive to you. Other babies will seem depressed and withdrawn, and will not look you in the eye. Despite your attempts, you simply may be unable to soothe or comfort the baby. Still others will suffer from minimal weight or height gain. Babies suffering from drug-related problems, due to prenatal exposure to drugs or alcohol from their birth mother's pregnancy, may also suffer from prolonged crying, as well as being startled easily. Often, these babies will also be over-sensitive to lights and sounds, as well.

As a foster parent, it is important that you provide consistent physical comfort to a baby suffering from these symptoms. In order for him to develop healthy relationships, he will need you to hold him in your arms, providing love and warmth. In fact, your foster baby will require a great deal of hugs, kisses, and physical contact from you. By doing so, you will help him to learn how to develop trust in others. Speak to him often, in a warm and pleasant tone, and with positive words of love and comfort. Encourage him to be social, to interact with you and others; engage him in eye contact. It will also be important for his senses to develop further. Find ways for him to use all of his senses: hearing, sight, smell, taste, and touch. Try to allow him to experience each of these every day.

Toddler: 1–5 Years

- Develops and masters motor skills

- Unsteady in his emotional state; may throw tantrums for seemingly unnecessary reasons

- Learns to play with others

- Attention span generally increases

- Learns to dress himself

- Becomes toilet trained

- Continues to learn through senses

- Becomes sensitive to others' needs

- Becomes very active and energetic

- Very curious: asks "why" a great deal

- Imaginative

- Aware of what is right and wrong, and develops understanding of consequences

This is the age normally associated with "The Terrible Twos." For many parents, it can be a trying time, as it exhausts the patience of even the most patient of parents. For foster children who have come from abusive homes, this developmental stage can be even more draining. A foster child exposed to abuse and neglect may be overly aggressive: answering back to you with the continuous reply of "no," yelling and screaming in defiance, and even becoming physically defiant with kicking, hitting, and throwing of objects. He may act openly defiant towards you, as he struggles with feelings of hostility towards his birth parents at such a young age. Aggressive behavior is not uncommon with foster children at this age, and can often result in tantrums of some sort. He might hit, bite, kick, shove, or show other forms of outward aggression towards you or others. He may even turn his aggression upon himself, as he inflicts pain onto himself through hitting, slapping, pulling of hair, or even banging his head.

Foster children in the toddler age of development may have great difficulties with attachment. Indeed, he will most likely have trouble distinguishing between you and his birth parents or biological family members. You may find your young foster child is withdrawn or distant when you speak with him. Your foster child might cling to a toy or stuffed animal. He may experience strong feelings of insecurity. This insecurity may produce feelings of abandonment whenever he might leave your presence, causing him to cling to you tightly whenever you leave. Panic might set in when he is separated from you. Bedtime or naptime may also be times where he feels strongly unsettled, causing him to become anxious and thus having a difficult time getting to sleep. He might also simply refuse to go to sleep, due to feelings of anger and resentment.

His cognitive development might be delayed due to the abuse or neglect he experienced before coming to live with you. His speech patterns and use of vocabulary might also be delayed. You might find his maturity level hindered, as he acts in an infantile manner. Eating may also become burdensome, for both you and him, as he might simply refuse to eat. He might also hoard his food, hiding it in his bedroom or other locations. If he has been sexually abused, he might show inappropriate sexual behavior for his age.

You can help him with these challenges in a number of ways. Provide for him additional nurturing. Do not allow him to regress to a younger age level, but instead encourage him to act his age, congratulating him when he acts like "a big boy." Or, if need be, allow him to act at a younger age level if he has missed out on early parental affection, and needs to receive the care he might have missed. (If you are unsure how to proceed, talk this over with the child's caseworker who should be able to advise and support you. A doctor or other professional may also need to be consulted.) Find areas you can compliment him in, giving him a sense of achievement. Provide a safe environment for him, ensuring that your house is childproof and secure. Teach him how to take care of himself with toilet issues, as well as brushing his teeth, combing his hair, and washing himself. Assign him small chores around the house. This will not only give him a feeling of accomplishment, but also a feeling of belonging. Assist him in dressing, and show him how he can dress himself. Expose him to new places, experiences, and people. Engage him in activities that allow him to strengthen his motor skills, such as forms of drawing, running, climbing, and other activities. Finally, engage him daily in communication, and encourage him to express his feelings openly and honestly with you.

School Age: 5–12 Years

- Appetite increases

- Likes to play with peers

- May begin to lie, or tell on others

- Becomes sick more quickly due to exposure from illnesses at school

- Becomes more private around adults

- Very active physically

- May become more argumentative as he seeks his own identity

- Highly competitive

- Sensitive to own shortcomings and personal failures

Over one third of the children in foster care in the US are between the ages of 5 and 15, with the average age being 10 (Child Welfare League of America 2005). While some of these children are placed under foster care supervision for the first time, many more suffer from multiple placements. The more a child is moved from home to home, and from placement to placement, the more difficult it is for that child to place trust in someone. Disturbingly, some of these children may come to believe that they are unwanted, unloved, and unimportant. They may lash out to their foster parents and other adults as a result. Along with this, schools may be a place where they also do not feel they belong, causing problems in their educational journey, too. Like all children, they wish to be loved, and strongly want a family to belong to.

Those children between the ages of 5 and 12 who have suffered from abuse and neglect tend to cling to adults. Even though they enjoy being around others their age, their peers, they truly want to be around adults and parental figures. This includes you, as a foster parent. You may find that your foster child in this age group wants to be with you at all times. He may cling to you when you leave, interrupt conversations with others just so he can be heard, and will seek to find acceptance in your eyes. He may worry about visiting with his own birth parents, as he might feel that he has to choose between the two of you. Some foster children struggle with the feelings that they are betraying their own biological family by not only living with you, but coming to enjoy the time with you and love you, as well.

These children also may tend to feel insecure, and take this insecurity out on over-eating. Often, foster children over-eat, and gorge themselves on large amounts of food. Breakfast, lunch, and dinner time may become times where he tries to eat anything placed in front of him. At the same time, anorexia may be a result of his insecurity, too. His self-esteem might be quite low, as he denies himself any sense of accomplishment, refusing any praise given to him. Learning disabilities are common in foster children who fall into this age group, and he might have difficulty adjusting to his new classroom environment, as well as to his teachers and fellow students. Your foster child may also have intense bouts of anger and frustration at the situation he is in, and will probably not know how to properly handle his emotions. Defiance, aggression, and destructive behavior may result. Those children who have experienced sexual trauma may also express interest in inappropriate sexual behavior, or become more sexually mature than children their own age.

One of the ways you can help your foster child is to have him meet with a counselor on a regular basis. Talk to his caseworker about setting up regular appointments with a trained youth counselor who can help him understand the feelings he is having. Encourage him to share his feeling with you, the caseworker, and a counselor. Speak to him one on one daily on a personal level. Find out what he is interested in, such as hobbies, sports, and other activities, and find ways in which he can participate, giving him your full support and encouragement. See that he exercises on a regular basis, whether it is through sports or through some fun outdoor activities at your own home. As he probably came from an environment that did not provide for him healthy eating habits, make sure you provide for him a nutritious diet, and encourage him to eat healthy snacks. When his body begins the process of puberty, answer all of his questions, and see that he gets plenty of sleep each night. Find appropriate chores he can do at home, which will give him a sense of responsibility, trust, and a sense of belonging. Help him with his school work, and communicate with his teachers on a regular basis. Encourage him to make new friends at school. After checking with their parents, encourage him to invite them over to your home for friendly visits and supervised play time. Most of all, speak to him in positive terms, build up his self-esteem, and give him plenty of love.

Teens: 13–18 Years

- Completes puberty
- Growth spurts most common; he will probably reach adult height by the end of teen years
- Understands he is a sexual being, and may experiment sexually
- Begins to consider his future
- Will want to sleep more
- Will seek greater independence from adult figures; may become moody
- Concerned about body and clothing image
- Influenced more by friends and peers
- Will question authority; may become more argumentative

Each stage of development can be difficult for a foster parent, but perhaps the teen years are the most challenging. This is an age when teenagers try to find their own identity, and is often a time where teens try to "cut the apron strings," so to speak, in an attempt to gain self-independence. If he has been in the foster care system for some time, he will probably have moved from placement to placement. Years of anger, frustration, sadness, loneliness, and broken trust will be difficult to break. You will have to have great patience with your foster teen, as he struggles with conflicting emotions as well as his role and place within your family.

Trust is one issue he will have a very difficult time with. Whether this is his first placement, coming directly from his birth parents' house, or whether he has had multiple placements, he may feel that the adults in his life have betrayed him. He has lost everything he knows and loves, and is now in a strange home with people who are not his parents. He will build up walls around himself, in an attempt to safeguard his feelings. You are likely to have a hard time breaking through these walls, and trust will be difficult to establish, as he believes that he has no reason to place trust in you. Lies and mistruths are often common with foster teens, and you will have a difficult time knowing when he is sincere, and when he is misleading you.

As a result of being removed from his home, he may have anger towards adults, and express that anger towards you. He may challenge your rules and expectations within your home, and argue with you about them, resenting the fact that he is being forced to live with people he does not know. Your foster teen may try to break as many of your rules as he can, and make your life as miserable as possible, in the hope of you asking that he be removed from your home, believing that he will be returned to his biological family members. He may also seem very withdrawn and depressed, and may not wish to be included in any of your family activities, along with any sort of social interaction. He may not appreciate all you do for him, and will seldom thank you for meeting his needs, providing for him, and showing him kindness and love. As he has been placed into your home against his will, he may run away.

As his body continues to change physically, he will become self-absorbed. Hormonally, he will continue to develop, and his body will soon grow as he advances towards adulthood. Peer acceptance will be important to him, and he will seek to try to fit in with his fellow students. If he has moved often due to multiple placements, his school records may not be complete, and he may struggle in school. Learning disabilities may place him in a grade lower than other students in school, causing anxiety and embarrassment on his behalf. Behavior in school may also be challenging, as he lashes out in anger towards teachers and those in authority within the school.

Perhaps the most important step you can take in helping your foster teen is building trust with him. This will take time, and you will have to have patience; do not expect him to come to your home trusting all you say and do. Give him space and allow him time to learn to trust you. Do not make promises to him that you are not sure you are able to keep. Once a promise is broken by you, it gives him further evidence that he cannot trust you. Talk to him on a personal level; find out what his interests are and encourage him to pursue those. Show interest in him, as well as in his biological family. Help him enroll in after-school clubs and activities. Help him to research possible careers when he graduates from high school, and inform him that dropping out of high school will have severe negative consequences for him. Encourage him to express his feelings and emotions to you, as well as to a counselor, if necessary. He will need to learn that expressing his feelings is natural and healthy instead of keeping them inside.

Establish rules and consequences for your household as soon as possible. Assign him chores and responsibilities in your house, allowing him to feel part of the family as well as giving him a sense of importance and self-worth. As he will want to establish a sense of identity and independence from you and your family, allow him to be a teenager; give him permission to try to fit in with the other students at his school with clothing styles, as long as they are appropriate. Set up a homework station for him at home, perhaps at the kitchen table, and create a time when he is to attend to his homework each night, perhaps when he gets home, or after dinner. Let him know that you will help him with his homework as much as you are able to. Do not allow him to have computer technology in his room, alone and unsupervised.

No matter the age or ability of your foster child, he needs you. When you take a foster child into your home, you are making a commitment to "foster" that child. Remember, "foster" means to take care of, to help grow, and help develop another person. Your foster child may not express gratitude, return love, or show appreciation for what you are trying to do, but it is important to keep in mind that you are making a difference, a difference that could indeed last a lifetime.

CHAPTER 8

Foster Children and School

Laura, foster parent of four years

By the time my foster teen arrived at my house, it was her fifth foster home in six years. Due to many circumstances beyond her control, she had been bounced around from home to home and from school system to school system. Enrolling her into a new school was very difficult, for a few reasons.

Michelle was new to our county, and new to our caseworker, as well. The first difficulty was that her caseworker had no previous school records for her. When I arrived at our local high school to enroll her, I was unable to answer many of their questions. Did she have learning disabilities? Was she taking college prep courses or was she on a vocational track? How many high school credits did she have? Was she on pace to graduate on time? It was frustrating for all involved, and Michelle was unable to provide much information. She was confused, and it wasn't just because she was in a new school.

I spent many hours on the phone with the caseworker, and with her previous high school, trying to get the information she needed. By the time the transcripts finally arrived from her old school to the new one, Michelle had already been enrolled in her new courses. The school counselor at her new school found that she had already taken two of the classes she was now in, so she had to transfer to two new ones, wasting even more time.

Michelle had been through a great deal of trauma as a foster child. She had no contact with her biological parents or any members of her birth family, and we were unable to contact some of her previous foster parents. Not surprisingly, she had a difficult first few weeks adjusting to her new home and to my family. She didn't trust us, and she had no real reason to do so. After all, Michelle had been shuffled from home to home.

School was the last place Michelle wanted to go to each day. She had a hard time making friends and fitting in, as she was afraid that she would be moving to another home and another school soon. She was not focused on her classes, homework, or grades. Her teachers were not aware that she was a foster child until I made contact with them to check up on her. This was after we had received notices from the school that Michelle had been argumentative with her fellow students and some of her teachers.

After I established a relationship with her teachers, they were much more understanding of Michelle's circumstances, and were willing to work with her and allow some flexibility with her homework. Michelle needed to know that the teachers were on her side. She also needed to know that her teachers cared for her, as a person. One teacher, in particular, took her under her wing, and helped Michelle find some clubs and organizations to join. This opened up the door for Michelle to make some new friends. This teacher also encouraged Michelle to work hard in school, and to start thinking about life after high school. Without the help and understanding of these teachers, Michelle would likely have been another statistic of countless foster teens that drop out of high school, never graduating, and ending up on the wrong side of the streets.

Placement into a new home for a foster child certainly leads to many areas of emotional anxieties and stress. Foster parents and caseworkers recognize this, and are trained to help foster children with these issues. Yet, even more challenging for many foster children is the place where many spend most of their time each day: the school. Unfortunately, most foster parents and caseworkers have little knowledge or training to aid foster children while in school, and the schools may equally be unable to help.

In regard to both academic performance and positive behavior, foster children, in general, tend to perform below the level of those students who come from either traditional homes or economically disadvantaged homes. The majority of children under foster care supervision experience problems in behavior while enrolled in public schools. These behavioral problems may be indicated by feelings of aggressiveness, which result in aggressive behavior towards others. It has been found that children who are angry and frustrated are more prone to experience conduct problems. Foster children may also experience feelings of low self-esteem, delinquency, and disruptive behavior. They tend to be demanding and lack maturity as they seek the attention of those around them.

Foster children often have a difficult time with exhibiting proper school behavior during the school day. For many of the children, school is a constant reminder that they are, indeed, foster children without a true home. Their peers are living with biological family members while they are not. This can be a difficult reality for them, and can be manifested in several ways, such as displaying aggressive behavior, disruptive behavior, defiance, and low self-esteem. Some foster children simply withdraw and become antisocial, in an attempt to escape the current environment into which they have been thrust. For many foster children, violent behavior becomes the norm, as they act out in a negative and disruptive fashion not only in the school, but also in their foster home. This can prompt another move to another foster home and another school.

As a result of this behavior, foster children often face greater risks of suspension from school, affecting their academic standing. They may repeat a grade level, or simply be placed in classes that are not appropriate to their age level. Those children who suffer from depression have a much higher rate of behavior disorders, including violent behavior, which often results in school suspension.

New placements may translate to frustration and behavior disorders, due to the lack of stability in the foster child's life, as he or she endeavors to create new relationships on a continuous basis. Foster children often express these behavior problems because of the large amounts of school time missed with court appearances, doctors' appointments, or simply from multiple placements. High levels of absenteeism frequently lead to grade retention, which leads to frustration and behavioral problems. Those children who experience multiple placements may face the problem of not obtaining specific services to assist them with learning disabilities/impairments, as schools often do not have the time necessary to implement appropriate testing.

Many foster children wish to form strong, meaningful relationships with their teachers, but yet this is impossible if the child encounters multiple placements in multiple schools, resulting in frustration and possible behavior disorders. However, not only is a foster child's school performance affected by behavior disorders, but problems with emotional, mental, and health-related issues also affect school performance. Many children who are removed from their homes and placed into foster care enter the child welfare system with chronic health, developmental, and even psychiatric disorders, because of neglect and abuse they faced while in their birth homes. Add to this the emotional distress and suffering that occurs when the children are separated, or removed, from their birth parents.

Those foster children who were taken from homes due to neglect repeatedly suffer from a number of developmental delays (American Academy of Pediatrics 2000). These include poor language and vocabulary development, thus impairing communication skills. Antisocial behavior may result from neglect, and even poor brain development. To be sure, there are high levels of mental health problems with children under foster care, as discussed earlier in Chapter 5.

Sadly, many times these problems are not being addressed. Furthermore, psychological and emotional issues that challenge foster children may even worsen and increase, rather than improve and decrease, while under placement in foster homes and care. In many cases, at least in the US, foster children do not receive adequate services in regard to mental health and developmental issues, and are not likely to do so in the near future.

The majority of children placed under foster care supervision suffer from at least one learning-based developmental delay (American Academy of Pediatrics 2000). Additionally, these same foster children suffer from behavioral issues, as well. As many foster children encounter multiple displacements, it is highly likely that these students will receive neither the remediation nor the necessary services they require in regard to developmental delays. As indicated previously, foster children frequently suffer from language delay. Math and reading skills also appear to be weak within the ranks of foster children.

Indeed, foster children are at greater risk of struggling in school, both academically and socially, than those children who come from traditional homes, resulting in generally lower standardized test scores, poorer grades in school, as well as behavioral problems, often culminating in suspension from the school. Many children in the custody of child welfare agencies exhibit the need for special education services. In addition, students in foster care exhibit an array of academic difficulties, including cognitive abilities that are weaker than traditional students (Weinberg, Zetlin and Shen 2009). Federal and state funding to assist in this problem in the United States is lacking, and it is not likely that it will be addressed any time soon, as budgets continue to be slashed by child welfare agencies state by state, and across the nation.

A successful working relationship and collaboration may not exist between public schools, foster parents, birth parents, and child welfare agencies. Consequently, foster children do not receive the services they require in order to be successful. Yet, education is considered crucially important and vital for many foster children in regard to the quality of life they wish to have in their adult life.

School social workers, in general, have been ineffective in meeting the needs of those students who are foster children, yet the need is growing for these school employees to do so, as the population of foster children continues to escalate. Some caseworkers have, in the past, also neglected the school life of foster children, and ignored educational policies and procedures (DeGarmo 2012a).

Relationships between caseworkers and the teachers assigned to the foster children are often not as strong as they should be. Caseworkers often have difficulty in obtaining information in regard to the foster child's performance in the classroom. Schools are often reluctant to release this information to caseworkers, or are unable to do so because of legal issues. When this happens, caseworkers have to rely on you, as a foster parent, for information regarding the status of the child's progress within the school. Many times, this information from foster parents comes too late, and a failing grade is the result. Thus, caseworkers would benefit from easier access to the child's educational records, as well as consistent updates from the school. If more adults are aware of the foster child's academic performance and struggles, the chances are greater that an adult would be able to intervene and offer aid and assistance to the child before a failing grade results.

Teachers are often not made aware of the emotional challenges that foster children face. As foster children come with a myriad of emotional issues, many teachers are simply not equipped to handle these issues. Foster children may lash out in the middle of class while many teachers do not have the training or the resources to handle these challenges. Foster children often have difficulty with trust issues when it comes to adults, as well as building a healthy relationship with an adult figure. Thus, the relationship between teachers and foster children is quite often unhealthy. In the United States the rate of dropping out of school among foster youth is significantly greater than those students from traditional homes. Foster children who do drop out are also less likely to complete a General Education Development (GED) diploma (DeGarmo 2012a).

Teachers, as well as school counselors, often do not have the background information they might need when having a foster child under their supervision. In most cases, the background information is not permitted to be released due to issues of confidentiality through legal acts of protection. Yet, this information is often necessary for a teacher in order to understand fully the student's needs and abilities. The more information a teacher may have on the child, the better equipped the teacher becomes when trying to aid the child in his behavior and academic performance.

As indicated earlier, many schools are not aware that foster children are within their school walls. This is due, many times, to the caseworker involved with the foster child. In some instances, caseworkers simply do not get around to informing schools that a foster child has been or will be enrolled within a school or school district. This scenario already creates an obstacle and hindrance for the child under the care of the state, as teachers and school officials are not informed of any educational and special needs.

Foster Parents, Caseworkers, and Schools: A Team Effort

As foster children may spend more time with their teachers each week than with you as a foster parent, an individual teacher may have much more influence with the child. A special teacher may become a positive role model for your foster child. Thus, it is necessary for your child's teachers to have the tools and skills available to them in order to fully assist him. In order to do so, the relationship between the school, your caseworker, and you must be a strong one. Though a teacher will not be given all of the background information there is in regard to your foster child, for reasons of confidentiality, the child welfare agency will need to give as much information as possible to your child's school in order to fully deliver the aid he requires, as well as better understand the child's needs.

There are a number of ways in which foster parents and teachers can work together in order to help the foster child while he is in school. To begin with, teachers and foster parents need to develop reasonable expectations for the child in the areas of both academics and behavior. While these children may not live up to high expectations of them, they are able to make small strides while in foster homes, as well as in the classrooms. Foster parents and school officials must be cognizant of this, and encourage each and every success the child garners.

Second, your foster child strongly needs advocates while in school, those who are looking out for his best interests. He will benefit tremendously by a teacher helping him in the challenges that he faces each day in school. This might include help with homework and assistance in studying, as well as teaching him how to fit in socially and encouraging your foster child to surround himself with positive friends.

Along with this, the teacher can also aid your child by ensuring that all academic needs are met, making sure he is placed in the appropriate classes and receiving the proper testing environment.

Many foster children benefit from guidance counseling, and the teacher can aid in this by observing your foster child in the classroom and informing the school counselor and you of any emotional difficulties the child might be suffering from. Finally, the teacher can also help foster parents with any concerns and questions you might have in regard to your foster child, as well as deliver regular academic updates via electronic mail and phone calls to the home. As a foster parent, you will need to reach out to the teachers, and ask for as much information and updates as possible. It is essential to your child's success in school that you become actively involved and interested in your child's school life. Look for ways to volunteer in the school. Encourage your foster child to become active in after-school activities. Take an interest in your child's school work, and make sure it is done to the best of his ability each evening. Help your child study, and praise him when he does well. If you have a young foster child in the early years of school, read to him each evening, or listen to him read to you. Help him with his spelling and writing skills.

As foster children are often behind academically, as well as struggling with the fact that they are coming from outside school districts with different expectations, teachers in your child's school need to be conscious of the fact that he is a foster child. Foster children struggle with many personal and emotional issues while in the foster home, and homework is often not the main objective while in the home each evening. Instead, the emotional issues your child faces may take center stage on a particular evening. Teachers need to assign homework with this in mind, being sensitive to their issues. Let your child's teacher know this, and ask that they cooperate with you on this. Meet with the teachers, the school counselor, and perhaps even an administrator of the school when you enroll your foster child, and explain these concerns to them. It is highly likely that they have not had much experience with foster children, nor the challenges they face.

A support team comprising teachers, foster parents, and caseworker is essential to the academic and behavioral success of the foster teen. When all three work together as a team, your foster child will benefit. You, though, will probably have to take the initiative in this. You may have to be the leader, and form a team. Once you have formed such a team, it must be maintained and given constant attention in order for the relationship to continue and prosper. Each of you can help to maintain it through the use of emails and internet forums, phone calls and phone chains, letters and mailing lists, and through the use of the evaluation form created by foster parents, caseworkers, and teachers, which can be used to assist in remaining focused on future meetings centered around the child. Higher-performing schools value a partnership with parents and members of the community, and countless studies show that the more involved a parent is, the more successful the child is. Your situation is very different, though, from the typical parent/child relationship. As a result, it is even more essential that you not only become involved, but that you take the lead.

CHAPTER 9

Working with Caseworkers

Shirley and Todd, foster parents of eight years

I was tired, and I was ready to give up being a foster parent. I had been fostering for about five years, and had several children come through my home during that time. I began to wonder if I was doing a good job as a foster parent, as well as with my own two small children. There were too many times when I felt that the rules placed upon foster parents by the child welfare agencies were not in the best interests of the children. I had also had some negative experiences with some of the birth parents, which left me with guilt. The sleepless nights with foster babies, the angry birth parents, the restrictions; I was finished. As soon I was done fostering the baby in my home, I was done with being a foster parent.

It was Patty, our foster baby's caseworker, who changed my mind. Patty was a great caseworker, and it was a real joy to work with her. She had such a wonderful positive attitude, even as she listened to my husband and I complain about what we didn't like about the foster system. Her patience with us, her warm smile, and her attitude really helped us during some difficult times. We needed someone to listen to us, listen to our concerns, and Patty never hesitated. She made us feel as if we were valued foster parents.

Patty was not only concerned about our feelings, she was also concerned about the well-being and future of our foster baby. Patty would check in with us often, to see how all were doing in the house, and if all was well. Patty was also quick to pass along any information or news about our foster baby. Whenever we had any questions for Patty, she was always quick to return any phone calls or emails. Whether it was a question about a monthly invoice, visitation with the birth parents, or getting some information or resources for additional yearly training hours, Patty took care of our questions and our needs as foster parents, and was ready to help at a moment's notice.

When it was time for our foster baby to return to her family, it was a very difficult time for us, a very sad time. Our caseworker was aware of this, and helped make this transition a little easier for our family. In fact, she has helped us keep in contact with the child, now many years later.

Working with our caseworker helped to restore my faith in the foster care system. She showed me that my job as a foster parent was needed, and that my husband and I were doing a good job. She made our job as foster parents much easier. I could not have done my job as a foster parent without her, and I have come to appreciate how important caseworkers are to the overall success and well-being of foster children, as well as for foster parents.

In order to be a truly successful foster parent, you will need to work closely with your foster child's caseworker. It is important for the well-being of your foster child that you work alongside the caseworker, and help to build an effective partnership and strong working relationship with your child's caseworker. With this strong relationship, the two of you will have a much better chance of guiding your foster child through the many difficulties and challenges he will face, as well as working together to see that his future is as bright and successful as possible. Keep in mind, your caseworker wants what is best for your foster child, as well as what is best for you. After all, without foster parents, caseworkers would not be able to place children into foster homes.

Caseworkers have a most difficult job, as they work in what is a difficult and stressful environment. While your foster child is your main focus in regard to the child welfare agency, caseworkers have a large number of children in their caseload. They will see, on a daily basis, children who have been abused and neglected. They will have the responsibility of taking a child out of a home, against the strong wishes of both child and parent, and in sometimes hostile conditions. They will be required to work with the birth parents, instructing them on how they can be reunited with their child. At times, caseworkers will sit in a courtroom, as attorneys and birth parents battle over the custody of a child. The amount of paperwork that corresponds with each caseload can be daunting, as well.

As government agencies are suffering from decreases in government spending, child welfare agencies have suffered immensely. Budgets have been slashed, caseworker positions are not being filled, and are in fact, being cut, and many US states have seen the reduction of work days, again due to budgetary reasons. All of this simply means more work with less money and time to do it in. With more and more children coming into foster care each year, across the nation, and with the shortage of caseworkers available, those caseworkers who are employed by child welfare agencies are finding themselves with more and more children to look after. Not only do the caseworkers look after foster parent and foster children, they are also responsible for working alongside the biological parents, as well. Along with this, caseworkers have to ensure that all legalities in conjunction with your foster child are up to date. Add to this the fact that they have to visit the home of each foster parent and child once a month, and have a mountain of paperwork ever before them, it is easy to see why many caseworkers do not stay in their jobs for long periods of time, as work burnout is common in child welfare careers.

Many times, the relationships between foster parents and caseworkers are healthy and pleasant. Yet, there are also times when the relationship between the two is difficult and strained. Some foster parents may feel that their foster child's caseworker is not concerned with their needs, as phone calls and emails are not answered right away. Remember, your child's caseworker may also be the caseworker for up to 60 other foster children. Time is something that caseworkers do not have in large amounts. As the two of you will be working closely together, for the sake of your foster child, there are a number of strategies you can employ in order to strengthen this partnership.

Open and Honest Communication

Like any healthy relationship, it is important that your relationship with your foster child's caseworker is an open one, and is built on trust and mutual respect. It is important that you share all information about your foster child with the caseworker. Be honest with your caseworker about any concerns you might have in regards to your child. If you see signs that your foster child is having trouble adjusting to your home and family, share these concerns with the caseworker. Perhaps you have seen troubling signs after a visit with your foster child and the biological family members. If so, let your caseworker know. If you are worried about a possible reunification with the biological family, express these worries to the caseworker. If your foster child should become sick, let the caseworker know, even if it is only a day at home from the common cold or flu bug. Caseworkers have the responsibility of documenting everything when it comes to each of the foster children in their caseload. Do not be afraid of holding any information or concerns. Instead, the more you share with the caseworker, and the more honest you are, the stronger your partnership will become, which only benefits the well-being of your child.

Take steps to develop lines of communication with the caseworker. Make sure you both have each other's current telephone numbers and email addresses, for both home and work. Plan ahead, if possible, for home visitations, as well as visitations with the birth parents. There will be times when you will need to make a request to your caseworker, whether it is for permission to take your foster child on a vacation, attend a summer camp, or perhaps even attaining some additional reimbursement for a Christmas present. If you work from the beginning in establishing a strong partnership, these requests will be easier to make, and have a better chance of being met.

Meeting with your Caseworker

You are likely to have a monthly meeting with your foster child's caseworker. These meetings are often held in the home of the foster parents, as the caseworkers like to view the foster child where he has been placed, your home. Other times, you may be required to drive your foster child to a meeting with his biological family. Before you meet with your caseworker, whether at home or another setting, make sure you are prepared beforehand. Have all proper forms and information gathered together which you might need for the caseworker. This includes any school progress and report cards, names and contact information for his teachers, calendar of upcoming events in your household, medical paperwork, receipts and invoices, and any other personal observations you may have noted for your foster child. Also have with you your foster child's medical information, such as doctor's name, address, and phone number, primary health care information, as well as any dates for future medical and dental appointments. There are times when your caseworker might wish to have the birth family accompany the child to an appointment, and some planning by you beforehand will help this to go more smoothly for all involved.

If you should be traveling to meet at a predetermined location, make sure that you arrive on time, and that both you and your foster child are dressed nicely. You may be meeting with the birth family, and you will certainly not only wish to look nice for them, but you will also want your foster child to be dressed and looking nice for his family. This does not mean business attire and dresses for you and your child, but it does mean not showing up in dirty clothing, jeans with holes in them, and old faded T-shirts. A nice clean pair of pants, button-up shirt, and nice dress shoes is appropriate, and presents a nice image for yourself, as well as the fact that your foster child is looked after and well taken care of in the eyes of the biological parents and family members. You surely do not wish to give the impression that your foster child is living in a dirty environment, and that he is not living in a safe and loving home.

Time Alone

Part of your caseworker's job is to observe your foster child, and how he interacts with your family. Your caseworker has the responsibility of ensuring the foster child's health, safety, and well-being. Your caseworker is going to want to take some time to talk with your foster child. It is important that you give your foster child and caseworker privacy and space. Encourage your foster child to open up to the caseworker. After all, your child's caseworker is probably one of the few consistencies in his life at the moment, a person that he will see on a regular basis and a connection to his birth parents, family, and life before he came to be placed with you. Help your foster child to develop a strong and positive relationship with his caseworker in his own way. When your foster child leaves your home, whether it be through reunification or some other means, he will probably still remain in contact with his caseworker. Thus, it is important to his mental health that his relationship with his caseworker is a good and productive one.

Be an Advocate

Foster children often have no one to fight for them, stand up for them, or even look out for what is best for their future. In other words, they frequently have no advocate. Your foster child will need you fighting for them, as an advocate. Yet, it can be difficult being an effective advocate, while still maintaining boundaries and remaining professional in regard to your relationship with your caseworker. Some foster parents become so emotionally involved with their foster child that they become overly defensive or protective when they do not agree with the caseworker or child welfare agency's policies. Others may take personal offence while working with a caseworker, and as a result, no longer cooperate or offer information with their foster child's caseworker. What many foster parents forget is that they are not in control of their foster child's situation, nor control the outcome of where their foster child may end up living when leaving their home. It is therefore very important, for all involved, that you remain professional as you advocate for your child.

As an advocate, you have the right to be heard in your role as a foster parent. Your foster child needs someone standing in his corner, so to speak. When he is enrolled in a new school system in your area, he will need you to work alongside his caseworker, ensuring that he is in the right classes. If he has learning disabilities, he will need you to make sure that the right phone calls are made, the right teachers are informed, and the right testing is administered to him in order to determine how best to meet his learning needs. If he comes back to your house after meeting with his birth family, and is emotionally confused, he will need you to inform his caseworker about the turmoil he is facing when visitation occurs. If your foster child is in need of some kind of therapy, he will need you to insist that a therapist is assigned to him.

As caseworkers are often overworked, your foster child's needs may not be met right away. In fact, you may find that his needs are not being met at all. Your foster child will need you to persevere, and not give up. Your foster child will also require you to remain optimistic, even in the most difficult of times. At times, it will mean you being unwilling to take no for an answer, and not settle for second best. It may require you to "think outside the box," as you and your caseworker work together to create other ways to solve problems that he faces.

Your foster child's caseworker has a great deal on her plate. She has to look after the concerns and needs of not only your foster child, but also many others. There are also the other foster parents that she has to meet with each month, too. Along with that, she has to work with the birth parents, as well as attend countless court hearings. With a little preparation on your behalf, as well as organization and a positive attitude, the working relationship between you and your foster child's caseworker will be a pleasant and productive one.

CHAPTER 10

Birth Parents and You

Jim, foster parent of 12 years

Visit at my house, with the birth parents? I am sure there are a lot of "what if" thoughts going through your mind right now. Remember… birth parents are people too! In the past 12 years of being a foster parent, my family and I have met quite a few birth parents. Imagine a 13-year-old mom with a medically fragile baby, and no support from her biological mother. Someone needs to teach her how to care for her baby. We were blessed to be a part of helping her learn some of the most basic care tips. We were also able to keep in touch with the mom and son once they were reunified.

There are many opportunities for you to attend court hearings or reviews as a foster parent. I would encourage attendance whenever possible. In most cases, meeting the birth parents will relieve both foster and birth parents. When I meet the birth parents, I simply try to be myself, be considerate of what they are going through (the loss of their child) and encourage them to work on the case plan while I provide love and care for their child. I always talk to them about their child returning home. It is not my decision, of course, but reunification is the ultimate goal. Once they realize that I am on their side and want to help them be reunited with their child, they often soften up. If they have never met me, they may picture me in their mind as the person that "took my child." If I can remove that hostility from the start, and encourage them, that's a great start. Will this always work? Not necessarily, but in most cases…yes.

I will also say: working with the birth parents is not always easy. My husband and I have four biological children of our own. When we began to foster 12 years ago, we had NO intentions of adopting any children. Our goal was to give them a loving, safe environment and help them transition back home, or to an adoptive placement when appropriate. Thankfully, we have been able to do both, successfully.

We are currently in our first situation in which we really feel in our hearts that the child we have in our home currently could be a part of our "forever family." This is difficult! We are constantly refocusing ourselves to the ultimate goal of reunification/relative placement. We must remain focused and positive when we talk to the birth mother. I take lots of pictures on most visits, and give copies of the pictures to her mother. I have even made her a beautiful picture album with over 100 pictures. The birth mom loves her child and lights up when we share these gifts with her. Fortunately, she doesn't feel threatened in any way by the love our family has for her daughter.

Birth families love their children and the children love them. We want to help them get through whatever tough times they are facing. Of course, every situation will be different. Not every birth family will be receptive to you, and working with that family may not be an option. Keep an open mind and you never know what might happen. Each child, each situation, and each family is different. You will always hold memories of the children that have entered your home. Those memories will last forever, even when the children move on.

It can be difficult enough having a foster child in your home. He may have been placed in your home because of abuse or neglect from his family. Perhaps he was in danger from parents who were abusing themselves. Whatever the reason for his placement into the child welfare's custody, your foster child has most likely come with some emotional problems, and is struggling with the loss of his family. As a foster parent, it is part of your job to help your foster child deal with these issues, and help him adjust to his new environment, as well as develop a positive and loving relationship with him.

What can be more difficult, though, is another part of your role as a foster parent: co-parenting. When a foster parent shares the nurturing of a foster child alongside the birth parents and caseworker, reunification tends to happen at a quicker and more successful rate. Co-parenting sees you, as a foster parent, working alongside the biological parents of the child living under your roof, and with your family. This may be the more difficult part of your job. To begin with, these may be the people who abused or neglected your foster child. Helping them might just be the last thing you wish to do. Therefore, it is important that you do not prejudge them before you meet them. Indeed, your first inclination may be that these are people who do not deserve to have their child back. What is important to consider, though, is that many biological parents of foster children were abused themselves, and know of no other way when raising children. Also disturbing is that some birth parents were foster children, as well, and are just repeating the cycle they went through as a child. Certainly, there are reasons why their children are in care that we may never understand. What is best for your foster child, though, is that you work alongside your caseworker, as well as the birth parents, and try to determine what is best for your foster child's future, as well as how to best meet his needs in the present.

There are those biological parents who will be happy to work with you. They will not only be eager to work alongside you in order to be reunited with their child, but may also wish to learn how to better their parenting skills from you. They will appreciate that you are taking care of their child, and will be grateful for all that you do for him. You might be providing many more opportunities for him than they were ever able to do themselves, such as clothing, medical care, and material items. They may be grateful that he is in a house that has enough food for him, as well as appreciate that he is in a clean and safe home. These birth parents may even be thankful that he is in an environment where their child is getting a better education.

There are also those families that are angry with the child welfare agency, and feel that their child was taken away unnecessarily. What's more, there are those birth parents that are resentful of you for having their child placed in your home. They may see you as the enemy, the bad guy, and find fault with all you do. These biological parents may even verbally assault you in a meeting with the caseworker, or in front of their own children. Sadly, this type of situation turns some foster parents off from fostering more children, and drives them away from the system. Again, it is important to keep in mind that these biological parents are hurting themselves, and are struggling with their own personal issues. Lashing out towards you may be the only way they know to release their frustrations.

Many child welfare agencies have recently begun to ask for foster parents to become more involved with birth parents. Caseworkers are asking foster parents to reach out to birth parents through phone calls, emails, and face-to-face meetings. Child welfare agencies are encouraging both foster parents and birth families to work alongside each other in the hope of reuniting child and family. Not only will the foster child benefit from this improved relationship, but it is hoped that the biological parents may also benefit, as they learn positive parenting skills from the foster parents. There are a number of strategies that will reduce the stress you, as a foster parent, can use when working with birth parents.

Role Model

A few years back, controversy was stirred when a professional athlete, Charles Barkley, stated that he was not a role model. Unfortunately, this is not true for you. As a foster parent, you will be a role model for countless people, as many eyes will be upon you. Not only will you be a role model for your foster children, but also for the public as a whole. Foster parenting will be on display for all to see as you undertake your role as a foster parent. Perhaps others will be impressed by your role, and will wish to become a foster parent as well, or, at the very least, help out.

For birth parents and family members, though, you might be the best example of what a good parent is. Everything you do as a foster parent will send signals to the biological parents on how a parent should act, as well as how to treat their own children. When your foster child meets with his birth parents for visitations, he should be well dressed, clean, healthy, and looking his best. His hair should be combed, nails cut, clothes fitting nicely. After all, you are sending a message that he is worthy of your best attention and care.

Your foster child probably wants nothing more than to return home to his family. In fact, reunification is often the end goal for most foster children. Indeed, two thirds of all foster children who enter into custody are reunited with their parents. The longer a child stays in foster care, the less likely it is that reunification will be achieved. As a foster parent, part of your mission is to support reunification with your foster child and his biological parents. Do your best to encourage reunification between the child and his parents. Find ways you can help the biological parents with their parenting skills. Discuss ways and ideas on how you can help them work on their case plan, as they attempt to meet the requirements of reunification.

Questions

Upon meeting the birth parents for the first time, there are bound to be questions from both you and the birth parents. Your foster child's family members will want to know what kind of family their child is living with, what his home life will be like, if he is being taken care of, and many other concerns. After all, their child has been taken away from them, against their wishes, and placed in a strange home. They will have many concerns, and may not be as courteous to you as you might like. Be prepared for them to be hostile, rude, angry, or even distant. Remember, they are hurting, and have been through a traumatic experience with the removal of their child. Respectfully encourage them to ask you as many questions as they would like. It is important that you answer their questions as honestly and as openly as possible, treating them with the utmost integrity, kindness, and politeness. After all, you are modeling good adult behavior to them, as well as to your foster child.

Your foster child's biological parents and family members will know him better than anyone, and your meeting with them will offer you the opportunity to learn a great deal about him, as well as acquire important information you might need. When you ask questions about their child, you are showing the birth parents that you are interested in him and his well-being. By indicating, with your questions, that his parents are the experts, you will begin to form an important relationship, one that will benefit all involved. A list of questions prepared beforehand will help you gather the information you need. These questions might include:

- Is he on any medication?

- Does he have any allergies?

- Has he had chicken pox?

- Are there any medical concerns?

- Does he have any learning disabilities of any kind?

- What range of grades does he usually earn?

- What are his favorite subjects in school?

- What subjects does he struggle with?

- If he is from outside the school system, what school did he go to? (This will help you to gather all current school information, and ensure that his new school receives it.)

- Does he have any behavior problems?

- Does he have any fears?

- Can he swim?

- What are his favorite foods?

- What are his interests?

- If he is young, does he have a favorite toy?

- Does he have any particular religious practices?

- Does he have a regular routine at home?

Your Family

Your foster child's family will no doubt be very curious about you. If they have not already asked questions about you and your family, take time to share with them some information. Let them know that you are excited to have their child in your home for the time being. Tell them about some of the traditions in your home. Reassure them that their child will not only be safe in your home, but cared for and given plenty of positive attention. The more assurance birth parents have that their child is in a good home, the better the relationship will be between the two of you.

Visitations

Visitations are those scheduled, face-to-face meetings between a foster child and his biological parents, or family members. These visitations are considered by many to be the main factor in bringing about reunification between the child and parents, the end goal for foster parenting. Meetings are held in a central and neutral location: a community park, a church, a child welfare agency. During this meeting, your caseworker, or other social worker, is permitted the opportunity to assess the foster child's relationship with his parents or family members, and determine how the parents are progressing in their level of readiness for possible reunification. Visitations also allow the opportunity for parents to practice parenting skills, which the social worker will also assess. Those parents who attend visitations on a regular and consistent basis are more likely to be reunified with their child.

For foster children, visitations have many positive attributes. To begin with, your foster child's visit with his biological family members is likely to reduce his sense of abandonment by them. It is to be hoped that his sense of self-worth and importance will be bolstered, as he feels reassurance from his parents that they continue to love him, something he may very well doubt and struggle with internally. By expressing his feelings to them, he may continue to heal emotionally. His birth parents may also reassure him that he is in a good home, with you, and that he needs to listen to you, and follow your rules, thus strengthening his own relationship with you. In fact, those children who visit with their birth parents on a regular basis are less likely to exhibit behavioral problems in your home and in school, as their level of anxiety decreases, as they become better adjusted to placement within your family.

As positive as some visitations can be, they can also be times of confusion and dread, for both the foster child, as well as for the foster parents. It can be most heart wrenching for a foster child to arrive at a central location for visitation, only to wait for birth parents never to show. Other foster children may meet with their parents, yet have them speak negatively about the foster parents. Some may struggle with feelings of loyalty to both you and his birth parents. Still other foster children may be given false hope from their family members, hope about imminent reunification. Many of these foster children will return to their foster homes confused, frustrated, depressed, or full of anxiety. Misbehavior may increase in the home, as well as in school, as the child struggles to understand their parents' behavior. As a result, some foster parents come to dread visitations, as they feel they have to pick up the emotional pieces from the visits or, for some, start again from the beginning with their foster child. If your foster child should come back to your home feeling sad and confused, take time to allow him to talk to you and express his feelings about his visit. Try to answer any questions he might have, to the best of your ability. If necessary, refocus him on your house rules and remind him that he is important, and that he is loved by you, as well. Inform the caseworker immediately of any negative experiences or other concerns you might have from a visitation.

When possible, try to involve yourself in meeting the birth parents on a regular basis. Send recent pictures of your foster child along with him to the visitations for the family members to keep. These pictures can include birthday parties, school events, holidays, and other important events the parents are missing out on. Provide school reports, grades, and ongoing updates on his education. If you feel comfortable, encourage the parents to call your home, perhaps once a week, or allow your foster child to call the family. When your foster child sees you working alongside his own family members, or co-parenting, his emotional well-being will be strengthened, as well.

As a foster parent, it is important to remember that your foster child's biological parents are people in need. There are reasons why their child is in foster care, and under your supervision. These parents may lash out at you and the caseworker. They may have treated their own child in cruel and horrible ways. Yet, they still deserve your kindness and sympathy, not your anger. By working with them, and by showing them kindness and compassion, you will not only help them, you will teach your foster child an important lesson in love and humanity.

CHAPTER 11

Protecting Yourself and Your Family

Paula, foster parent of two years

I think your family's welfare is of the utmost importance. Foster children have an entire government agency focused solely on their welfare. Your family has you. The love and care you give to a foster child must not come at the expense of your own family.

I'd like to share with you some of the most important questions that I think the child welfare agency asks foster parents. What behaviors are you willing, or unwilling, to accept in a foster child? What age range are you interested in? How many children are you willing to accept? I cannot emphasize enough how crucial it is that you be totally, soul-searchingly honest in your answers to these questions. If you have a child of your own at home, as we do, it is vital to their safety and well-being.

Let me illustrate with one of our own experiences. Three beautiful children were placed in our home: two little girls and one little boy. They seemed perfect for our family! They were all younger than our six-year-old son, which meant that he couldn't be overpowered physically. They had no history of sexual abuse, which meant that our son wouldn't be a victim of them possibly sexually acting out.

Unfortunately, the children had been sexually abused, but no one knew it. The little boy, who shared a room with our son, tried to touch our son one night. I thank God that our son was older and stronger and was able to stop him! How differently things could have turned out if our son had been younger and weaker than the foster child. The little boy and his sisters needed extensive professional help and were removed from our home.

Remember, your family's well-being positively affects the well-being of the foster child. In order for fostering to be a success, it must be a success for everyone involved.

Taking children into your house can certainly be a challenge. Behavioral issues, learning disabilities, emotional trials; all can be exhausting and trying for a foster parent. Yet, what many foster parents often overlook is the risk factor that goes along with taking a foster child into a home. As a foster parent, you become vulnerable to many possibilities, and it is important that you protect yourself and your family from the possible implications and investigations.

Foster parents are more than twice as likely as birth parents to be the subject of a child maltreatment investigation (Minty and Bray 2001). Though most allegations of abuse and neglect by foster parents are found to be untrue, or unsubstantiated, these allegations are made, nonetheless. Foster parents have a higher chance of false accusations being made against them than birth parents (Minty and Bray 2001). These false accusations may stem from a variety of ways. First of all, those foster children who have come from environments of abuse and neglect may not recognize that the home and environment you are providing is a safe and stable one. The abuse and neglect they felt, themselves, may be all that they know, and they may simply make an allegation against you unknowingly, or unwillingly, due to past experiences. Other foster children, coming from the same type of environment, may make an allegation against a foster parent in the hope of leaving your home and being able to return to their own biological family. Other children may make an allegation as an attempt at distancing themselves emotionally from you, and setting up an emotional barrier or wall between themselves and foster families. Finally, some foster children may make an accusation of abuse or neglect in an attempt at gaining revenge on either the foster family or the biological family.

As a foster parent, you may also be at risk from birth parents or biological family members. False accusations of abuse, neglect, or other forms of maltreatment may be reported against you out of resentment by the family, as the child is living with you instead of a biological parent or family member. Along with this, false allegations might also be made against you out of jealousy, or simply in an attempt to justify the birth parent's own present, or even past, behavior.

The foster care system is commonly one that is misunderstood by society. Many in the public are not aware of the roles and responsibilities of foster parents, nor truly appreciate and understand why a child might be placed into foster care. Along with this, many people do not recognize the challenges that both foster children and foster parents face, with behavioral, emotional, and learning issues. As a result, someone in your area may mistakenly file a report to your child's welfare agency, or to law enforcement, doing so with good intentions, but false information.

Information Prior to Arrival

Prior to your foster child's arrival, there are several things you can do to protect yourself and your family from the risk of false accusations and allegations. Before the foster child is ever placed in your home, insist on getting all the information about the child that is available. This should include any history of emotional and behavior issues, learning disabilities, medical needs, as well as any physical or sexual abuse the child might have been subjected to. Ask about the visitation schedule; who he will be visiting with and how often the visits will occur. If the child has been placed in previous foster homes, try to obtain information regarding any possible false allegations or unsubstantiated reports made by child, birth parents, or other biological family members. Find out why the child was moved from the previous foster home and placed into yours. Ask to speak to the previous foster parents in an attempt to find out more about the child, along with his needs and concerns. Whenever possible, attempt to get all of this information in writing, whether from the caseworker, court system, or schools.

Written Records

Throughout the placement of your foster child in your house, it will be necessary to keep written records, a journal, or some sort of documentation. This written account will help you keep an accurate account of the time your foster child lives in your home. It is important that your writing is done in a manner which is observational, descriptive, and that it is a non-biased account of your foster child. Furthermore, you will want to make certain that your written account does not include your opinions. If you wish to include your opinions and feelings about him, you might wish to start a personal journal for yourself about his time with you.

Begin a journal about your foster child, beginning with his arrival. Explain the state of dress, behavior, and emotional well-being when he arrived. Describe his progress and daily events in your home. If he becomes sick, include this in your written records: the time he was sick, as well as how it was treated, including doctor visits and any medicine that you gave him. Document any changes in behavior he might exhibit, when he began behaving in this way, as well as the length of time he spent in this behavior. Detail how you addressed this change in behavior, and how he reacted to any rules and consequences you put into place as a result of misbehavior. Keep a notebook specifically for his school work, including grades and report cards, any behavioral problems or discipline, and any conversations held with teachers, school counselors, administrators, and other school employees.

Visitations are an important factor in the life of your foster child as well as his biological family members. Keep an account of every time he has a visitation, including the date, times, and locations of each visit. If he has significant emotional or behavioral changes after these visits, do your best to describe these in full. Any contact you have with the birth parents and biological family members should also be documented. You should also document each conversation you have with his caseworker. If he should display any serious conflicts or unusual behavior towards his biological family or caseworker, or even towards himself, document this in detail, and report it to the caseworker immediately. If you suspect any kind of abuse while visiting his family, take before and after pictures of him as another form of evidence.

Safety

As your foster child is under the custody of the state, you are liable for his safety and well-being. It is important that your entire family knows this, including your own children. There will be times when he will not be able to join your own children in some activities, as some states have rules against trampolines, certain water activities, and other endeavors. Sit down with your family and discuss safety issues such as medicines locked away in cabinets, seatbelt fastening while in moving vehicles, electrical outlets, and other concerns. It will be important not only for your foster child, but also for your entire family that you routinely inspect your home for any problems that could bring harm or danger to those living in your home. Check fire alarms, electrical outlets, locks, windows, and other features on a consistent basis. Keep a fire extinguisher in your home for emergencies, and make sure your foster child knows what to do in case a fire should begin in your home.

Supervision

Supervision of your foster child is a must at all times. You will be held responsible for his whereabouts and safety, and may be held accountable if he should come to harm. As indicated in Chapter 6, it is not only important that you know where your foster child is at all times, it is essential. If your foster child should wish to visit a friend's house or another home, do a thorough check of who lives there, the environment he will be in, and the level of safety and supervision he will be under. Be sure to call the parents of the home he wishes to visit, not only to ensure that the environment is a safe one, but also to express any concerns about your foster child you might have with them. If you feel that the friend's home environment is not a safe one, do not be afraid to say no to the foster child. You will also need to be certain that all after-school functions he participates in are closely supervised, before giving him permission to take part.

The supervision of your foster child is also necessary in your own home. Like many children, it might be unwise to allow him to play unattended at any time. If he is in his room playing or even napping, make sure that his door is open, if just a little bit. From time to time, check in on him, and make certain that he is OK and not doing anything that you would disapprove of. If he is in the back yard, make sure that he will come to no harm out there from stray animals, sharp objects, unwelcome visitors, or by simply wandering off by himself. Again, you will wish to periodically check in on him from time to time, while he is outside. If he is rather young, you will want an adult out there with him, at all times. Whether he is inside your home or outside, make certain that there are not too many places where he might hide himself. Some children might escape into a world of imagination and fun by hiding, while others might hide in an attempt to escape the harsh realities they have faced, or do so out of anger and resentment towards an adult. Make sure you know the locations of all the places your foster child might hide, and try to eliminate as many of these as possible.

Sexually Active Children

You may foster a child who has been sexually active in the past, due either to his own choices, or to his having been sexually abused by others. Perhaps the child is currently sexually active, or is one who has been exposed to sexual behavior prior to his placement within your own home. Whatever the scenario, you must take extra care in protecting yourself from false allegations and possible accusations from the child. Whenever you are in the same room with a foster child who has sexually related problems, it is imperative that you have another adult in the room with you at all times or, at the very least, nearby and within listening distance. This will not only protect you as a foster parent, it will also protect your child from making any false accusations.

Disturbingly, those children who have been previously abused sexually are more likely to become a victim of sexual abuse again. If your foster child should make a new allegation that he was sexually abused, take this seriously, and report it to your caseworker immediately, and without hesitation. Even if he has a history of making false accusations, it is your duty and responsibility as a foster parent to protect him from harm. By reporting all accusations from him, you are also protecting yourself, as well.

Discipline

As a parent, you have your own approach for disciplining your own biological children. These methods may have to be different, though, for your foster child. When disciplining your foster child, you may have to come up with different methods of discipline, in order to protect yourself. Quite simply, you are never allowed to use any form of corporal punishment on a foster child. You are not permitted to spank your child at any time. Do not threaten it as a form of discipline, either. Even the suggestion of it could place you at risk. Instead, find other alternatives for punishing your foster child. Discuss these with him, and explain to him what is and is not permissible, and all consequences he will face if your rules are broken. If possible, also discuss these with your caseworker, and even the birth parents, if they are receptive to you. If you find that your foster child is so out of control that he must be restrained in order to not only protect those around him, but to protect himself, as well, do so only if you have had proper training in restraint techniques, as you do not want to accidentally harm him, or give him cause to falsely accuse you of doing so.

Abuse, Threats, and Injuries

Abuse can take different forms: physical, emotional, sexual, and verbal. If you suspect that your foster child has been abused in any way, contact your caseworker immediately, and file a report. An investigator will be assigned to investigate the claim before taking any further action. If your home should fall under investigation, answer the questions as openly and honestly as you can, sharing as much information as you know with the investigators. If you should withhold any information, it will only make it more difficult for all involved.

Any time a child talks about suicide, it should be taken with the utmost seriousness by you, and reported to the caseworker immediately. Sometimes, foster children may threaten suicide as an attention-seeking device, hoping to bring attention to themselves. Even if you should suspect that this is the case, you still must report it to the caseworker as soon as you are able to do so. As the child's emotional state may be unstable, an attention-seeking threat can quickly result in serious injury or death to the child. All letters and notes that indicate a suicide threat should be collected and given to the caseworker. Close and constant adult supervision needs to be provided to your foster child if he should threaten bodily harm or suicide.

If your foster child should sustain a serious injury or suffer from a severe illness in your house, at school, or anywhere else outside your home, report this to the caseworker, as well. As the child is not legally yours, but is instead in the custody of the state, your caseworker will be required to report any and all injuries and serious illnesses in their reports. You will need to report any injury or serious illness immediately to your caseworker.

Noting incidents such as injuries, illness, and abuse in written documentation will benefit your memory when recounting information to caseworkers and possible investigators, and will help to protect you and your family, as well. Regular reports to your caseworker will also help to protect your family. The foster parent who does not take seriously a threat of possible harm to a family is only setting himself up for serious legal implications and possible endangerment to the entire family.

CHAPTER 12

Finding Help as a Foster Parent

Lynne, foster friend of two years

For several years, I observed a family in my church becoming foster parents. I watched from afar as the family hosted several children for varying lengths of time. I prayed for the foster family and prayed for each of their foster children by name. I felt guilty as I thought about all the reasons I could not assist with foster parenting—travel associated with my job, frequent visits to my elderly parents almost four hours away in a neighboring state, being available for my own children who live in yet another state. Sometimes I would cook dinner for the foster family or offer to provide Santa gifts for the foster child(ren) in the home. Surely there was more I could do to support foster parents!

I asked my foster parent friends to think of some way I could provide encouragement and support to foster parents. Thanks to my friends, I have discovered several ways to participate in foster parenting other than actually serving as a foster parent, and this discovery has had a huge impact on my life. I arrange for dinner and child care for our local foster parenting group during their bi-monthly meetings. I have become involved and been trained to participate in Safe Havens, a service at my church which provides supervised visitation opportunities for foster children and their parents allowing foster parents to have a small break. I am exploring being trained to provide respite care for foster parents. Of course, none of these efforts come close to the commitment of actually serving as a foster parent, but I know now that I am doing what I can to share in the care of these most precious and worthy children in our community—those children in foster care.

Foster parenting is hard work! It may just be the hardest work you ever do. You will often find yourself exhausted, both mentally and physically, and feel drained. There is very little money available to help you, and you will not be reimbursed for all the money you spend on your foster child. The job will require you to work 24 hours a day, 7 days a week, with no time off. You will probably feel overworked and underappreciated. You will work with children who are probably coming from difficult and harmful environments. Some of these children will have health issues, some will come with behavioral issues, and some will struggle with learning disabilities. Many times, the children you work with will try your patience, and leave you with headaches, frustrations, disappointments, and even heartbreaks. There is a reason why many people are not foster parents, as it is often too difficult. The turnover rate for foster parents in the United States is between 30 percent and 50 percent each year (U.S. Department of Health and Human Services 2005).

When foster parenting becomes too stressful, you, your family, and your foster child will all feel the effects. Thus, one of the most important reminders for you, as a foster parent, is the fact that you need to take care of yourself, physically, mentally, and emotionally. If you neglect yourself, your family will suffer as a result. By taking the following stress-reducing steps, you will help to ensure your well-being, as you care for others in your home.

Time for You

First and foremost, you need to make time for yourself. As a foster parent, this will be difficult, as you will be required to take care of a child full time. Along with this, you may also need to care for your own children, as well as your spouse. You may have a full-time job that requires a great deal of your energy, plus there are those other commitments you have, such as church (or temple, etc.), volunteering, and other organizations you might be involved in. Finding time for you will not be easy, but it is essential. Make time to do something you enjoy, and that you find relaxing. Spend time with some friends, perhaps over lunch or dinner. Do not neglect your own personal health; make sure you get plenty of exercise regularly and eat healthily.

Your Marriage

Sadly, many marriages or partnerships suffer during the fostering process. When you are putting much of your energies and time into your foster child, you may be so drained and exhausted that you soon neglect your spouse or partner. Also, some foster children are skilled at pitting one parent against the other, bringing some heated and very unproductive arguments to your home. Make sure that you and your spouse or partner are on the same page with your parenting, and ensure that the two of you are consistent when it comes to all decision making with your foster child. Finally, do not neglect the needs and concerns of your spouse or partner. Instead, make your relationship the cornerstone of your home, and work to make it a productive and happy one.

Your Children

If you have children of your own, you may find that you are not giving them the attention and love they need. Instead, your attention is many times on the needs and behavior of your foster child. As a result, your relationship with your biological children can suffer. Make sure you spend one-on-one time with each of your own children. Go out on a "date" with them, take them for a drive, have a picnic. During this time alone, allow them to talk to you about how they are feeling about the foster child in your home. If they are frustrated, encourage them to tell you about how they feel. Listening to your child is important to your relationship. After all, they may be worn out and exhausted, too, just like you might be.

In order to be the best foster parent you can, you will need to come to the understanding that you cannot do it all by yourself. There are a number of agencies, organizations, and resources available to foster parents, all in the attempt to help make the foster parenting experience a little easier.

Respite

There are those times when foster parents will require a short-term break from their foster child. This break may be the result of foster parents traveling on vacation, a temporary move into a new home, or it may be that the birth children in the foster home require some much-needed time with their own parents. Along with this, respite may be used simply because some foster parents are trying to prevent burnout, and need a break from their foster child. Other foster parents are often used for respite, as they are officially licensed to look after foster children, and will be reimbursed for the interim that the foster child is placed in their home, during the short break.

Respite for your foster child can be a difficult and confusing time, if not prepared for in advance. Foster parents can make this short-term transition a much smoother one, and create less stress for them, if they follow a few simple guidelines. To begin with, when seeking respite, contact your caseworker in advance, allowing a few weeks' notice for your caseworker to find a placement for your foster child. If you have the opportunity, visit the family with the foster child beforehand. This will allow you to ease the concerns and fears the child might have, especially if your foster child has attachment issues. Make plans with the respite family about the best time to drop off your foster child, as well as when you would like to pick him up after the break is over.

As you pack for your foster child, ensure that he has enough clean clothes, shoes, toothbrush, comb, and so on. If your foster child is a baby, make sure you pack extra diapers and baby wipes. If your child has a special toy, or stuffed animal, place this in his suitcase, along with some photos of his birth family, and some of him with your family, as well. If he has any special medication, make sure there are ample supplies of it packed, as you do not want the respite family having to purchase some while your foster child is with them. If he is old enough, give your foster child your phone number, and let him know that he can call you anytime there is an emergency. During the time he is away, call him on the phone on regular occasions. While calling, speak to the respite family, checking with them to see if there are any problems or concerns you can help them with. Rest assured, respite is a welcome break for many foster parents, and is an opportunity that you should not feel bad about taking. It is a normal part of the foster care process, and allows foster parents the opportunity to recharge, as well as destress.

Foster Parent Support Groups

There are a number of foster parent support groups and associations across the nation. A few of these organizations may be national ones, while many others are local groups without paid staff comprising foster parents, like you. Either way, you will benefit from being in a support organization, as they will provide you with support, information, fellowship, and important insights that will help you be a better foster parent. To find a support group in your own area, contact your local child welfare agency for information, or search for one online.

Support groups and associations offer you the opportunity to develop relationships with other foster parents. These relationships are wonderful occasions for you to validate your own experiences and the emotions you feel as a foster parent. Fellow foster parents will also be able to discuss common experiences and common concerns related to the foster children living in their homes, as well as share ideas and resources with each other. No one will truly understand and appreciate what you are experiencing and feeling than other foster parents.

Many associations meet once a month, while others may meet every other month. It is important that you attend these meetings, as it keeps you connected with other foster parents, and the resources they might have, and many associations include training during their meetings. Training will take several forms: CPR certification, drug and alcohol awareness, behavior modifications, and so on. The hours spent in training will go towards the yearly amount of hours needed in order to remain certified as a foster parent.

Churches

Many churches, temples, mosques, and other places of worship across the nation have opened their doors to foster parents in an attempt to help them as they care for children. Indeed, many local foster parent associations meet in local places of worship each month. There are those churches or places of worship who have trained some of their members in order to supervise visitations between foster child and biological family members, with the meetings held within the place of worship itself. Other ways some have helped foster parents and their foster children include:

- Collecting new or donated clothing, toys, bedding materials, and other necessities for foster children.

- Encouraging church members to become mentors to foster children.

- Hosting foster children who have aged out of the foster care program, and are no longer living in a foster home, or helping to pay for rent and accommodation for the teen.

- Donating school supplies and backpacks for foster children.

- Donating to a foster parent fund, helping to support local foster parents.

- Helping to pay for summer camps and field trips for foster children.

- Setting up a fund in order to aid former foster children in their college and post-high school education.

Additional Aid and Assistance

If you were to take a quick look through a book store or library, you would quickly find that there is not much information available for foster parents, or for the entire foster care program, in general. To be sure, there is some, but the amount of material and resources available to a foster parent is certainly not a large one.

In the age of the internet, foster parents across the nation can connect, like never before. There are a number of foster parent websites where foster parents can gather and share information, resources, and so on. Many of the websites resemble nationwide support groups and associations, with the exception that they are online. In the traditional form of literature, there are a few foster parent magazines published throughout the year. Along with this, there are some books for foster parents, as well as about the foster care program, in general. The Resources section has a list of resource materials available for foster parents, including web addresses and other contact information.

CHAPTER 13

When a Foster Child Leaves

Kelly, foster parent of 12 years

"I could never do what you do, because I could never give them back." That is the phrase I hear most often when I tell someone I am a foster parent. I agree, giving the children back is undoubtedly one of the hardest parts of being a foster parent. The day a child arrives and the day a child leaves are the most difficult days.

Arrival day is a little easier on me. We always bake cookies because I believe the smell of freshly baked cookies does the best job of helping a child feel welcomed and comfortable. Don't get me wrong, most children don't come in excited to be at our home. In their minds, we are not rescuing them. We would be selfish enough to think that these children are lucky to be here and we dare to believe we have rescued them. From their perspective, however, we are scary strangers, the unknown, and nothing that they are used to. They, like any other child, simply want to go home, cookies or no cookies.

Like children tend to be, foster children are resilient, and by Day Two, they honestly do feel more at home and usually begin calling us Mom and Dad within 48 hours, if it takes that long. The fact that the children settle in so quickly is what makes the leaving part more difficult. They settle quickly because of a simple routine of unconditional love, food, regular sleep, and safety: simple things that almost all of these children have not previously experienced.

There have been children that I have NOT been so sorry to see leave. I can think of two out of the couple of dozen children that we have had that I have had their bags packed and ready by the door before a child welfare agency car ever pulled in the driveway. Granted, these children were going to safe places and we didn't have to worry about them, which always makes it a little easier. Mostly, however, it is a horrible dark and ever looming day that I usually hope never arrives.

I remember looking into the face of an eight-year-old girl who had been living with us for 18 months, and taking her slender arms and saying, "I am so happy for you, your aunt and uncle seem so nice, I know you will like it with them." I lied. We didn't want her to go but our hands had been tied by the state of Georgia and she was leaving.

"OK, Mommy, I love you," she said with a smile on her face and tears in her eyes. "Goodbye, sweet baby girl." I kissed her for the hundredth time and walked away as instructed and got in my car. I was brave for about two miles and then I had to pull over to the side of the road and sobbed until my tears dried up. My heart still has not healed all the way from that one episode and it has now been almost ten years since that goodbye. It is just one of many heartbreaking, teary goodbyes.

Everyone is right; we don't ever want to give them back.

Perhaps one of the most difficult aspects of being a foster parent is the moment when your foster child leaves your home. As a foster parent, your home becomes a place where foster children come for a period of time, with the goal of being reunited with their family in the near future. Reunification is not possible for some foster children, and the birth parents' rights are terminated. As a result, these children become available for adoption, and some foster parents do indeed end up making their foster child a permanent addition to their family through adoption. If reunification with the birth parents is not possible, many foster children instead are placed into a birth family member's home. Whatever the reason might be, reunification can be a difficult time for foster parents, as the child they have come to love leaves their home.

Each foster child is different, and each placement into a home creates different sets of emotions. As a foster parent, there may be those children you do not have strong attachments to, due to emotional or behavioral issues, yet an attachment with these children is still made, nonetheless. Some foster children will be so difficult, that you may even ask for them to be removed. Still, other foster children will steal your heart, and will become a dear and cherished member of your family, leaving you heartbroken. When any foster child leaves your home, no matter the level of attachment, there will be emotions when it is time to say goodbye, for both you and the child.

Reasons for Removal

There are indeed several reasons why a foster child might be removed from your home. Over 50 percent of foster children are reunited with their parents, while roughly 10 percent will go to live with other members of the biological family, such as aunts and uncles and grandparents (AFCARS 2012). Eighteen percent of foster children will end up being adopted, while fewer than 10 percent will age out of the foster care system upon reaching the age of 18. Some removals are usually due to a court decision, and can come rather suddenly. Perhaps, the level of care needed for the foster child is beyond your ability, and the child is placed in another environment where his needs can be better met. Your foster child may have been separated from his siblings when first placed into your home. If a foster home is found later on which can, in fact, provide care for all of the children, your foster child may leave your home and be reunited with his siblings in the same home. The closure of a home as a foster placement may be another reason for removal.

As a foster parent, you might request for the child to be removed from your home. Possibly, your own children and foster children are simply not getting along as you had hoped. Perhaps, you feel as if your foster child is harmful to your family, or is a dangerous influence on your children. You may find that you are unable to care for him properly. Another reason for removal may be that your foster child is refusing to follow your rules, or is extremely disruptive. When requesting that a foster child is removed from your home, meet with the caseworker before you make any final decisions, and see if any of your concerns can be positively addressed. If this fails and removal is imminent, give the caseworker plenty of notice, in order to ensure that the best possible placement is found for the child. Along with this, work with the caseworker in trying to ease the transition from your home to another placement. To the best of your ability, try to reduce your foster child's anxiety about moving from your home.

Removal

There are times when the removal of a foster child may come suddenly, and without any prior warning. You may only have a few days, or even a few hours, before your foster child is to move. This may be due to a court order, health reasons, or placement into another foster home. Other times, plenty of notice is given to the foster parents beforehand. Whenever you are told, there are sure to be emotions involved, for both you and the foster child. The removal of a child may be a joyous event or one that is filled with grief. If the removal of your foster child is one that you disapprove of, due to his new placement, it is important that you do not share these feelings with your foster child. If you must express your concerns and feelings with the caseworker, do so in private, as it will only serve to burden him with more anxiety during this difficult time of separation.

Rest assured, many foster parents do feel grief during the removal of their foster child, as the child has come to be an important and loved member of their family. Whenever a loved one leaves home, emotions of grief and sadness are normal. Other times, though, a foster parent may be angry with the removal, as the parent may feel that the new placement is not in the best interest of the child. Pointing this out to the child will only upset him further. It is necessary for you, as a foster parent, to remember that you are not in charge of the situation, as difficult as it may be. The removal of foster children from a home is often a decision that is made in the court.

How your foster child is told that he is leaving can be a difficult conversation. You and the caseworker need to decide how best to inform the child. If the foster child has a special relationship with the caseworker, it might be best if the caseworker lets him know. Maybe the foster mother or father would be best suited to tell the child, due to the relationship built between the child and the parent. Whoever should be the one to tell your foster child needs to do so in a way that is marked with care, sincerity, kindness, and honesty. As there are a number of reasons why your foster child might leave your home, it is important that you be honest with him about his leaving in terms and words that he can understand, and at his level. If he is excited about returning to his home and his parents, celebrate this with him. Perhaps have a going away party, and celebrate his time with you. If he is concerned and full of anxiety about moving to another foster home, an adoptive one, or even about moving back to his own home, speak to him in positive terms, keeping a positive attitude with him. Remind him that he is an important person and that you care for him and want the best for him.

If you have children of your own, they may be confused as to why your foster child is leaving, or concerned about where he is going. Share this with your caseworker, and she may be able to help you answer these concerns and questions to your own family. Talking with your own children about the departure will help to ease any worries your own family has. Remember, they may also go through the grieving process, as well, as their foster sibling has lived alongside them for the duration of the placement, becoming an important part of their lives, as well.

Stages of Grief

Grief can be expressed in a variety of ways, depending upon the individual, as it is personal. Some will shed tears and cry while others will hold it inside. Some will busy themselves in a task, while others will seem detached and far away. The departure of your foster child from your home can be one that is devastating to you and your family. A brief look at the stages of grief, based upon Kübler-Ross's work of 1969, is important in order to understand fully the feelings that may come along with the removal of your foster child from your family. These same feelings may have been felt by your foster child when he was removed from his own home, and first placed in yours.

Shock

The removal of the foster child may bring feelings of shock to the foster family. After a family member has formed an emotional attachment to the child, the sudden removal may cause deep shock and uncertainty, leaving the foster family confused.

Denial

With a sudden departure, some foster parents may deny that they ever formed a relationship with their foster child, or feel any sadness towards the removal. Even though they deny these feelings, they grieve believing that they were unable to provide the help the child needed.

Anger

A foster child's removal from a foster parent home may bring feelings of anger and severe disappointment with the caseworker, as well as with the child welfare agency system. Foster parents may blame the system or caseworker for the placement of their foster child into an environment they feel is not productive, or even harmful to the child.

Guilt

During this stage, foster parents may experience feelings of guilt, blaming themselves with the belief that they are at fault, and try to comprehend what they did "wrong" in the removal of the foster child. Still other foster parents may experience guilt if they were the ones asking for the removal, as they were unable to continue caring for the child.

Bargaining

Some foster parents will try to substitute the grief they have with helping others in need, in an attempt to justify the loss of their foster child. Others will try to substitute the loss with the placement of another foster child in their home, hoping that this new placement will help them forget about the child that just left.

Depression

There are different components to depression brought on by grief. Some foster parents will become easily irritated; others will experience a constant state of feeling tired. Others will feel as if they can no longer continue with their day-to-day lives, and have a difficult time with the tasks associated with family, friends, work, and marriage.

Acceptance

After the passage of time, the grief from the loss of the foster child decreases, allowing the foster parent to accept the removal of the child, and move on. The emotional well-being of the foster parent improves, and a sense of understanding of the child's removal becomes clearer.

Preparing for the Move

Because this can be a time of great difficulty and one of emotional upheaval, it is important to prepare beforehand when it comes to the transition of your foster child from your home into another. From the very first day you bring a foster child into your home, it is critical to remember that he will very probably not be with you forever. There will come a time when he will move to another home, whether it is reunification with his parents, his family members, another foster home, or adoption. Therefore, planning for his departure begins when he first arrives.

Lifebook

One of the ways you can prepare is by organizing a lifebook for your foster child. This book can be a wonderful healing tool for your foster child as he moves to a new home. For some children, a lifebook is the only reminder they have of previous houses and families they once called home. Essentially, a lifebook is a scrapbook of your foster child's life, and is something he can take with him to his new home, and throughout his life. Sadly, when many foster children are placed into a foster home, much of their early life story is lost, and can never be retraced.

When designing a lifebook for your foster child, make sure you include him in creating the book. Do your best to trace his early life; ask your caseworker for information, try to retrieve early pictures and information from birth parents and family members, if possible. Add pictures of the birth family, when possible, as well as any other foster parents he might have had. Include pictures of his friends and other important people in his life. Be sure to identify each person in the pictures. If you have any certificates of any kind that he might have earned or received, include these also. Letters from important people in his life would also be a great addition to his lifebook. Also, be sure to include any medical history you can locate. You may need help from his caseworker, along with his birth family, if possible. Any family history you can add would also be very beneficial to him, both now and later on in life. This might include military service, education, and accomplishments of not only his birth parents, but of his biological family members, as well. Don't forget to add information about his own interests and hobbies, with plenty of pictures of him engaged in activities. Finally, leave several blank pages in the back of his lifebook, so he can add pictures, information, and even his personal thoughts later on as he grows, or perhaps even in his next foster home.

The New Family

Your foster child will certainly be full of questions about where he will soon be moving to. He might be moving back home with his birth parents, or members of his biological family. Perhaps he is moving to another foster home, or is being adopted by another family. Try to find out as much information about the situation as you can. If possible, acquire the phone number of the family he is moving to from your caseworker and call them ahead of time, introducing yourself to them. Allow your foster child to speak with them, getting to know them a little before the move. If permissible, arrange for a visit with the family, along with the caseworker, allowing all sides the opportunity to meet face to face. During this visit, discuss any parenting practices you might have in common, as well as any differences in house rules you might have. This information will help to prepare your foster child for his new home, as it might help to answer some of his questions, thus easing the transition a little. Afterwards, you may find that the caseworker arranges for overnight and weekend visitations with the family, allowing your foster child the occasion for a smoother transition from your home to theirs.

During the Move

This is generally a time of great anxiety for all involved. Your foster child may be experiencing excitement, concern, sadness, or even fear at the prospect of leaving your home and moving to another, depending on the placement. You may experience the same feelings, too. How you handle his departure from your home to his new one is an important factor in how he handles the transition.

Regardless of how long he has been with you, reassure your foster child that you have enjoyed having him live with you. Tell him that the time spent with him is important to you and your family, and that he is important, as well. Sit down and reflect upon some of the enjoyable memories that you and your family shared, as well as some of your positive feelings you have for him. Point out any positive steps and challenges overcome that he might have dealt with while living with you. Often, foster children come from environments and homes where they are not shown love, or not told that they are important. You might be the first person to tell him that he matters, that he is important, and that he is cared for and loved.

Think about throwing a going away party for your foster child as an opportunity to show him how much he will be missed. Invite the caseworker, those you know from your place of worship, if you have one, friends of the family along with his friends, and anybody else who played an important part of his life with you.

Perhaps you could give him some going away presents that he might remember you by. Make it as fun a party for him as you possibly can, again showing him that he is cared for.

Packing for him can be emotional, as it may bring back memories of being removed from his previous home. Personally reflect upon the time he arrived at your house. It is likely that the few belongings he had were in a black plastic bag. Perhaps he was dirty when brought to you, and had an unkempt appearance. Emotionally, he was probably scared, confused, and unsure if he was ever to see his family again. How you pack for him will be important to his well-being.

First, make sure he has a suitcase, or suitcases. It does not need to be a brand new one; some foster parent associations or child welfare agencies may offer these for free. Second, nicely fold all of his clothing and belongings in the suitcases, including him in this. If he has a lot of toys or large items, you may have to use boxes for these. Make sure you pack everything he owns, including everything he came with to your home. Third, include as many group photographs of him with your family as possible. Pictures of you and your family may help him in the grieving process of leaving your home, and can serve as a valuable reminder that he is loved and cared for. Finally, place some self-addressed self-stamped envelopes in his suitcase so that he can write to you from his new home. Add some stationery, pencils, and pens, so that he has everything he needs to write to you. Also, include contact information for him, such as your address, phone numbers, and email address in his lifebook.

After the Move

After your foster child has left, you will probably have feelings of anxiety. It is normal to miss him, perhaps even grieve for him. As his former caregiver, you will wonder how he is doing, and will most likely have friends and family members of yours asking about him. He will have those same feelings and emotions in his new home. To help him in this time of transition, it is important to reach out and contact him. Call him on the phone and allow him to tell you all about his new home and new family. Encourage your own children to speak with him, as well. Write letters to him and send him pictures of your family and family events from time to time. Remember birthdays and other important events in his life, including holidays and school events, and send cards. If you live nearby, let him know when you can attend school functions and extra-curricular activities or programs of his. If possible, arrange visits for him to come to your house. Not only will he enjoy it, but his new family may certainly appreciate the break.

Saying goodbye is never easy for anyone, and may be especially difficult for you and your foster child. After your foster child leaves your home, you may feel like you never wish to foster again, as the pain is too great. The grief you feel may be overwhelming. On the other hand, you may feel relief when he leaves, as the time with him in your home was a difficult one. Whatever the circumstance, there will be emotions involved. With the right preparation, this time of transition can be a little bit easier for all involved.

CHAPTER 14

Adoption

Jason and Tammy, foster parents of ten years

Adoption can mean many things to many people. The legal meaning is: a legal proceeding that creates a parent/child relation between persons not related by blood; the adopted child is entitled to all the privileges belonging to a natural child of the adoptive parents. To me adoption is giving a child a sense of belonging to a family who loves and cares for them, who can give them a stable home life in order for them to grow and develop.

My husband Jason and I have adopted three beautiful girls. Two of the girls are siblings (Destiny and Amber). This journey was a long and hard one. The girls came to us when they were six and one and a half years old. They lived with us for two years in foster care. All through their stay, we were told by caseworkers and CASA [Court Appointed Special Advocate] workers that they would be recommending them to stay with us. In the end, the final decision was up to the judge. Judgment day came, and the judge ruled for the girls to be returned to their birth mother. Pain, anger, and depression came; it was so hard to understand. We are Christians and we know God has a plan, but I often ask why…

We would send letters, cards, and even tried to call, but never received an answer. During this time, we took in another foster child, six-month-old Shirley. Joy had come back into our lives, but we were still missing Destiny and Amber, and prayed daily that they were all right. We had visits with Shirley's birth mother and her birth father. Her birth father Roberto is Hispanic. After Shirley had lived with us for two years, Roberto called and spoke with me on the phone, telling me that he wanted Shirley to live with us. He wanted his daughter to have a better life and education. It wasn't long after that the birth mother said the same. Both parents had signed their rights away.

Today, we still see Shirley's birth mother a couple of times a year. Roberto has gone back to Mexico and calls every couple of months. Roberto truly loves his daughter, even after the adoption was final. He has been to church with us several times and spent holidays with us. He will always be a part of our extended family.

It was three years later when I received a call from Destiny and Amber's grandmother. The girls were living with their aunt and uncle. Their mother was in trouble and their dad in jail. The aunt and uncle had five children of their own living in a single wide trailer. My world came crashing down when I received the call. Grandmother asked if we still wanted the girls. Of course, I answered. The only question I had was how soon. I called the child welfare agency in the county they were living and told them they had been placed with us three years ago. They told us they could not move them unless the aunt and uncle decided they could not care for them. This went on for several weeks. I was able to contact the aunt and talk to the girls. The aunt and I talked a lot during this time and she finally decided they couldn't take care of all the children's needs. Two weeks is a lot of time on our knees praying that the girls were safe. We finally got the call; the child welfare agency would bring them to us. Instead, we told them that we were on our way to pick them up.

It wasn't very long after when their mother called us. During the next few weeks, we spent a lot of time talking on the phone. She was then placed into drug rehab, and we even visited her there. (It is important for the children to know their parents are all right.) Both parents signed their rights away. We talked to her weekly and visited about once a month.

The girls are now 15 and nine years old. Our extended family grows yet again. Both the biological mother and I are "Mama" and we tell each other we love each other and the children see that. Adoption isn't about leaving one family to be legally a part of another. It is about extending your family.

When a child is taken into custody and placed into a foster home, the intent is that the placement is to be temporary, with reunification the main objective. Yet, there are those instances when reunification is not possible, and the child is placed through the court system for adoption.

Of over 560,000 children placed in foster care in the United States in 2010, it is estimated that 107,000 became eligible for adoption. Sadly, only around 53,000 of these children were adopted during that year, with over half of these children being adopted by foster parents, with the rest being adopted by family members, and a small percentage being adopted by non-relatives (AFCARS 2012). For those children who are not adopted, many remain in the foster care system for extended periods of time. Some of these children are moved to group homes, while others simply age out of the foster care system, never truly finding a family of their own and a place to call home.

There are several reasons why a foster child might be placed up for adoption. First, the custody rights of the birth parents are voluntarily terminated; second, the custody rights of the birth parents are terminated by a court order; and third, the child is up for adoption due to the death of birth parents.

Recently, child welfare agencies have found that foster parents are the ideal people to adopt a foster child. After all, the foster family has been raising the child for an extended amount of time, meeting his needs, and nurturing him since he was removed from his birth parents' home. If he has special needs, the foster parents are familiar with these, and have gained valuable insight and resources to meet these needs. Adoption by his foster parents will also allow him to remain in the same school system, benefitting from having the same teachers who are already familiar with him and his needs. The child is familiar with his foster parents, and has formed a strong and meaningful attachment to them during the course of his placement within their home. As the child has come to live, laugh, and love with the family, he has probably become a member of the family, and will be able to legally stay with a family he has come to know and trust.

Indeed, there are advantages to adopting a child through the foster care system, and as a foster parent considering the adoption of a foster child, you will find these advantages most helpful. As a foster parent, you will have had no legal rights with your foster child, as the child has been a ward of the state, and under the state's custody. In fact, such simple tasks as having the child's hair cut may have been a decision that was out of your hands. As an adoptive parent, you gain full legal rights to the child, the same legal and parental rights you would have if he were a birth child of yours. Furthermore, all questions about medical, religious, educational, travel arrangements, and all other parental decisions will now become fully yours; no longer will you have to share decision making with the birth parents, caseworker, child welfare agency, and the state. All responsibilities of decision making will become yours with the adoption of your foster child.

Many times, adoption can be very expensive. Adoption agencies both inside the United States and around the world often charge large fees that are beyond most families. Adopting through the foster care system, though, is free of these high fees. In most states, both federal and state assistance programs are available to foster parents during the adopting process. Many states provide an attorney for the foster parents, thus making it even more financially beneficial. Even more helpful for adoptive foster parents is that most children under foster care supervision are already covered by the federal Medicaid assistance program, and may also become eligible for the same assistance from the state after the adoption process is complete.

Another advantage that adoptive foster parents have is that of time. They have had the time to become very familiar with their foster child. Any learning disabilities, emotional difficulties, and behavioral issues are known to the family, as well as his family background. Valuable insight and information may have been received from birth parents from previous meetings. Foster parents have had time to become aware of any concerns regarding the foster child, and respond to them accordingly. Along with this, the foster child has become familiar with the rules and expectations within his foster home, and has had time to adjust to his new home and new family. If adopted by his foster parents, he will not have to face the emotional turmoil associated with moving to yet another home. His friends, foster siblings, school, and even pets remain the same. All that he has come to know while placed in a foster home will remain consistent, helping to ease the transition that comes with every adoption.

With all the positive differences in adopting a foster child, there are some challenges associated with the process. In the US adoptive foster parents will find that, to begin with, the financial assistance they received each month when fostering is no longer available once the child becomes a legal part of the family. Indeed, once the child is adopted, these former foster parents will become responsible for all financial obligations; day care, clothing, extra-curricular activities will no longer be supplemented by the state.

Adoption can be an emotionally difficult time for a foster child. No longer will the child be able to hope for possible reunification with his biological parents, or even with other members of his birth family. Instead, the termination of rights by his birth parents might produce feelings of grief and loss within him, fears he had kept bottled within himself during the length of his stay in foster care. He may even feel that he has betrayed his biological family as he legally takes the adoptive parents' last name, as well as becoming a permanent member of the family. You may find that the child revisits the stages of grief again, both during and after the adoption process. Indeed, it can be an emotionally traumatic time for all involved.

The Process

In the United States the adoption of a child is a long and complex process. Sadly, for some foster parents, it may end up as a heartbreaking experience, as not all adoptions reach the desired conclusion. For all involved, the length of time the process takes, as well as the emotional roller coaster that foster parents and children ride on, can be emotionally overwhelming.

A foster child may come up for adoption after the court finds that reunification is not possible, usually after the child has been in care for 12 months. After this time has elapsed, the child welfare agency will begin a process entitled Termination of Parental Rights, or TPR, thus terminating the rights of the birth parents. Following this, the caseworker will conduct a thorough and exhaustive search for other birth family members in order to find a family member willing and able to adopt the child. If a family member should become available, he or she will have to undergo an extensive background check, including a police history and house evaluation, in order to determine if the child will be safe with the family member, and if the placement through adoption will be a healthy, stable, and secure one. This process usually takes an additional six months, though it can take much longer, sometimes lasting a year or longer. If there is no family member found that is able or willing to adopt the foster child, he will then be up for open adoption. At this time, you, as a foster parent, will be able to begin the adoption process.

As each state has different rules and regulations within the foster care program, it should come as no surprise that the adoption process is also different, depending upon state policies. Generally speaking, the next step for you, in the adoption process, is to let your caseworker know your desire to adopt. It is to be hoped that you have already discussed this with your caseworker, as it will make the time period a little shorter. Working alongside your caseworker, a petition needs to be filed with a judge. In order to accomplish this, a family or an adoption attorney will need to be hired. This will help you determine that all adoption and foster care laws are adhered to. Your attorney will also represent you during the adoption hearing process, and will help you fill out the petition forms, and file them within the court system. As petitions vary from one state to another, your attorney will be versed in your state's legalities and requirements.

During the petition process, you will be required to provide some background information about you and your spouse. This information may include details on why you are petitioning the court to adopt your foster child and why you wish to change your status as a foster parent to an adoptive one. The petition may also require information about the reasoning behind the termination of the birth parents' rights to your foster child, as well as a statement from you as to why you are the right and appropriate choice to become the legal guardian of the child. Finally, a statement may also be required indicating that your foster child's best interests do indeed lie in being adopted by your family.

As a foster parent, you were required to have a home evaluation, not only before you began, during your training, but also each year you are licensed as a foster parent. Even though you have had custody of your foster child for some time, at some point during the adoption process, you will be asked to undergo yet another home evaluation, due to state laws. Along with this, a family evaluation will be conducted, again according to state laws. Some state laws dictate that not only will you be interviewed by a representative of the state, but also that an interview may be requested from friends and family members of yours, as well, in order to determine if you are a fit and secure household for an adopted child. This portion of the process will most likely be a lengthy one, and will require a great deal of information from you. Your attorney should be able to guide you in this, answering any questions you might have.

After all paperwork has been officially filed, and all interviews and evaluations have concluded, your lawyer will formally notify all interested parties about the possibility of your foster child's adoption. This formal notification is required by state law, and is carried out in an attempt to locate any biological family member who might object to the adoption. If no biological family member comes forward, indicating that they wish to adopt the child, you will then be asked to appear in court. At this time, your attorney will represent you in front of the judge for the adoption of your foster child. The last step will lie with the judge; it will be the court's determination whether or not the child's best interests lie with foster adoption over foster care. If the process should reach this stage, it is likely that the adoption will be approved.

Post Adoption

Even though the last name on your newly adopted child's certificate of adoption reads the same as yours, there will still be many questions and concerns awaiting him, and you, in the future. In order for a healthy and successful transition from foster custody to legal adoption, there are a number of strategies you can use as an adoptive parent. To begin with, talk with him frequently about the process, step by step, and encourage him to ask questions and share any concerns he might have with you. He is likely to have concerns about never seeing his birth family again. It is important for you to remember that even though he now has your last name, he will still have very strong feelings about his biological family and background. The older he is, the stronger these bonds to his biological family will be. It is very dangerous for adoptive families to discount this background and his feelings towards them. Instead, recognize them as an important part of who he is, and try to incorporate them into his life.

Open Adoption

If possible, and if everyone feels comfortable with the idea, consider having an open adoption. An open adoption allows open contact between the biological parents and the foster child, allowing for the potential of a one-on-one relationship between both sides, as they interact directly with each other. Communication may consist of letters, emails, social networking sites, phone calls, and even visits. Open adoption benefits both sides, especially the child, as it permits him to resolve any feelings of loss and relationship, and gives him access to information that he might seek later on in life. These types of adoption also allow the child to maintain relationships and connections with people who are important in his life. Open adoptions are not for everyone, and serious consideration needs to be made before making a decision either way. Adoptions that are open with biological parents and children need to be made on an individual basis, as each adoption situation is different and unique.

Adoption Day

Adoption Day parties are a wonderful way to celebrate as your foster child officially joins your family. Invite friends and family members over on the day that you legally adopt him. Celebrate the event with cake, ice cream, balloons, and presents, making it similar to a birthday party. Let him know that this is a very special day not only for him, but also for your entire family, as it grows officially by one more with his adoption into your family.

Grief and Transition

The adoption of your foster child is indeed a joyous and happy occasion. Yet, the internal process for all involved can be a challenging one, especially for your child. He may have a difficult time accepting the fact that he will never return to live with his biological parents or birth family members again. It is necessary for you, as an adoptive parent, to allow your child time to grieve the loss of connection with his birth family. He may very well need time to experience the stages of grief before he fully transfers attachment from his birth family to yours. Even though he may have lived in your home for some time as a foster child, he will probably re-experience feelings of loss during the adoption process. Allow him to discuss his feelings of grief and loss with you as you listen attentively to him, validating his feelings and emotions. If he should ask any questions about his biological parents or birth family, answer them as honestly as you can. At the same time, help him to transfer attachment from his birth family to yours by ensuring that he is included in all aspects of your family and, when possible, incorporate parts of his previous family's traditions into your own, as it may help him to feel more comfortable. After all, his birth family gave him his appearance and gender, his intelligence, his temperament, talents, and of course, his life. These, of course, will never change.

There will be difficult times during the adoption process, and afterwards too. It may seem, at times, that your relationship is going backwards. Yet, with time, love, and patience, adoptions are often one of the greatest gifts of love you can offer a child; a gift that will bless your family, as well.

References

Adoption and Foster Care Analysis and Reporting System (AFCARS) (2012) *The AFCARS Report.* Available at www.acf.hhs.gov/sites/default/files/cb/afcarsreport19.pdf, accessed on 9 May 2013.

American Academy of Pediatrics (2000) "Developmental issues for young children in foster care." *Pediatrics 106,* 5, 1145–1150.

Child Welfare League of America (CWLA) (2005) "Quick Facts About Foster Care." Available from www.cwla.org/programs/fostercare/factsheet.htm, accessed on 29 March 2013.

Courtney, M. E., Dworsky, A., Ruth, G., Keller, T., Havlicek, J. and Bost, N. (2005) *Midwest Evaluation of Adult Functioning of Former Foster Youth: Outcomes at Age 19.* Chicago, IL: University of Chicago, Chapin Hall Center for Children.

DeGarmo, J.N. (2012a) *Responding to the Needs of Foster Teens in a Rural School District.* Ed.D. Dissertation, Walden University. Ann Arbor, MI: ProQuest LLC.

DeGarmo, J.N. (2012b) *Fostering Love: One Foster Parent's Journey.* Bloomington, IN: Crossbooks.

Federal Trade Commission (2007) "Children Not Seeing More Food Ads on Television." Available at www.ftc.gov/opa/2007/06/childrenadsstudy.shtm, accessed on 30 March 2013.

Kübler-Ross, E. (1969) *On Death and Dying.* New York, NY: Touchstone.

Lenhart, A. (2009) "Teens and Sexting." Washington, DC: Pew Research Center. Available at http://pewinternet.org/Reports/2009/Teens-and-Sexting.aspx, accessed on 31 March 2013.

Mayo Clinic (2011) "Children and TV: Limiting your child's screen time." Mayo Foundation for Medical Education and Research. Available at http://kcpt.org/wp-content/uploads/2012/01/Mayo_Screen_Time.pdf, accessed on 9 May 2013.

Mendes, P. and Moslehuddin, B. (2006) "From dependence to interdependence: Towards better outcomes for young people leaving state care." *Child Abuse Review 15,* 2, 110–126.

Minty, B. and Bray, S. (2001) "Allegations against foster carers: An in-depth study." *Child Abuse Review 10,* 5, 336–350.

O'Higgins, N. (2001) *Youth Unemployment and Employment Policy: A Global Perspective*. Geneva: International Labour Office; distributed by ILO Publications Center, Waldorf, MD.

Sherman, M. (2011) "Sexting not on the agenda; Teenagers rarely charged for photos." *Concord Monitor*, September 11.

Stein, M. (2006) "Research review: Young people leaving care." *Child and Family Social Work 1*, 3, 273–279.

Sullivan, A. (2009) "Teen pregnancy: An epidemic in foster care." *Time*, July 22.

Thoburn, J. (2007) *Globalisation and Child Welfare: Some Lessons from a Cross-National Study of Children in Out-Of-Home Care*. Norwich: University of East Anglia Social Work Monographs. Available at www.uea.ac.uk/polopoly_fs/1.103398!globalisation%201108.pdf, accessed on 9 May 2013.

U.S. Department of Health and Human Services (2005) *Understanding Foster Parenting: Using Administrative Data to Explore Retention*. Available at http://aspe.hhs.gov/hsp/05/foster-parenting/report.pdf, accessed on 9 May 2013.

U.S. General Accounting Office (1977) *Children in Foster Care Institutions—Steps Government Can Take to Improve their Care*. Washington, DC: U.S. Government Printing Office.

Weinberg, L., Zetlin, A. and Shea, N. (2009) "Removing barriers to educating children in foster care through interagency collaboration: A seven county multiple-case study." *Child Welfare League of America 88*, 4, 77–111.

Resources

Publications
Caring Magazine
P.O. Box 133
Swanley
Kent BR8 7UQ
Phone: 0845 120 4550
Email: info@ccpas.co.uk
Website: www.ccpas.co.uk

Foster Focus Magazine
608 Main Street
Watsontown, PA 17777
Phone: +1 570-538-3608
Email: info@fosterfocusmag.com
Website: http://fosterfocusmag.com/aboutus.html

Fostering Families Today
541 E Garden Dr Unit N
Windsor, CO 80550
Phone: +1 888-924-6736
Fax: +1 970-686-7412
Email: louis@adoptinfo.net
Website: www.adoptinfo.net/indexfft.html

Represent: The Voice of Youth in Foster Care
224 W. 29th Street
New York, NY 10001
Phone: +1 212-279-0708
Fax: +1 212-279-8856
Website: www.representmag.org

Online Training Programs
Foster Care and Adoptive Community
Phone: +1 818-998-4462
Website: www.fosterparents.com/states3

FosterParentCollege.Com
Northwest Media, Inc.
326 West 12th Avenue
Eugene, OR 97401
Phone: +1 800-777-6636
Fax: +1 541-343-0177
Email: fpc@northwestmedia.com
Website: www.fosterparentcollege.com

FosterParentTraining.Com
Website: www.fosterparenttraining.com

Other Resources

Adopting.org
Information and resources for those considering becoming foster
parents, for foster parents, and for those who were formerly fostered.
Support, training, money issues, transitions, and practical help.

Website: www.adopting.org/adoptions/considering-fostering-resources-
and-information-for-families-considering-foster-care-and-foster-
parenting.html

Foster Parent Network
A website designed to help foster parents. The site has information
about online courses, helpful weblinks, and support groups.
Website: www.fosterparentnet.org/default.aspx

National Foster Parent Association
National Foster Parent Association
2021 E Hennepin Ave #320
Minneapolis, MN 55413-1769
Phone: +1 800-557-5238
Fax: +1 888-925-5634
Email: info@NFPAonline.org
Website: www.NFPAonline.org

Foster Care Contact Information: United States (by State)

Alabama Department of Human Resources
Center for Communications
Gordon Persons Building, Suite 2104
50 North Ripley Street
Montgomery, AL 36130

Phone: 334-242-1310
Website: www.dhr.alabama.gov/services/Foster_Care/FC_Children_
Teens.aspx

Alaska Health and Social Services
350 Main Street, Room 404
P.O. Box 110601
Juneau, AK 99811-0601
Phone: 907-465-3030
Website: www.hss.state.ak.us/ocs/fostercare/default.htm

Arkansas Foster Family Services
P.O. Box 1437, Slot S560
Little Rock, AR 72203-1437
Phone: 501-682-1442
Website: www.fosterarkansas.org

Arizona Division of Children, Youth, and Families
P.O. Box 6123 Site Code 940A
Phoenix, AZ 85007
Phone: 877-543-7633
Website: www.azdes.gov/az_adoption

California Department of Social Services
744 P Street
Sacramento, CA 95814
Phone: 916-651-8788
Website: www.cdss.ca.gov/cdssweb/Default.htm

Colorado Department of Human Services
1575 Sherman Street, 1st Floor
Denver, CO 80203-1714
Phone: 800-799-5876
Website: www.colorado.gov/cs/Satellite/CDHS-Main/
CBON/1251575083520

Connecticut Department of Children and Families
Commissioner's Office
505 Hudson Street
Hartford, CT 06106
Phone: 860-550-6300
Website: www.ct.gov/dcf/site/default.asp

Delaware Services for Children, Youth, and their Families
1825 Faulkland Road
Wilmington, DE 19805
Phone: 302-451-2800
Website: www.kids.delaware.gov/fs/fostercare.shtml

District of Columbia Child and Family Services Agency
400 6th Street, SW
Washington, DC 20024
Phone: 202-442-6100
Website: http://cfsa@dc.gov

Florida Department of Children and Families
100 Opa-locka Boulevard
Opa-locka, FL 33054
Phone: 305-769-6324
Website: www.fosteringflorida.com/index.shtml

Georgia Department of Family and Children Services
2 Peachtree Street, NW
Suite 18-486
Atlanta, GA 30303
Phone: 404-651-9361
Website: http://dfcs.dhs.georgia.gov

Hawaii Department of Human Services
Hui Ho'omalu
680 Iwilei Road, Suite 500
Honolulu, HI 96817
Phone: 888-879-8970
Website: http://humanservices.hawaii.gov

Idaho Department of Health and Welfare
PO Box 83720
Boise, ID 83720-0036
Phone: 800-926-2588
Website: www.healthandwelfare.idaho.gov/Children/
AdoptionFosterCareHome/tabid/75/Default.aspx

Illinois Department of Family and Children Services
406 East Monroe Street
Springfield, IL 62701
Phone: 800-572-2390
Website: www.state.il.us/dcfs/foster/index.shtml

Indiana Department of Child Services
953 Monument Drive
Lebanon, IN 46052
Phone: 888-631-9510
Website: www.in.gov/dcs/index.htm

Iowa Department of Human Services
1305 E. Walnut
Des Moines, IA 50319-0114
Phone: 515-281-5521
Website: www.dhs.iowa.gov

Kansas Department for Children and Families
230 E. William
Wichita, KS 67201
Phone: 785-296-4653
Website: www.dcf.ks.gov/Pages/AgencyInformation.aspx

Kentucky Cabinet for Health and Family Services
Office of the Secretary
275 E. Main Street
Frankfort, KY 40621
Phone: 800-372-2973
Website: http://chfs.ky.gov

Louisiana Department of Children and Family Services
627 N. Fourth Street
Baton Rouge, LA 70802
Phone: 888-524-3578
Website: www.dss.state.la.us

Maine Office of Child and Family Services
2 Anthony Avenue
Augusta, ME 04333-0011
Phone: 207-624-7900
Website: www.maine.gov/dhhs/ocfs

Maryland Department of Human Services
311 West Saratoga Street
Baltimore, MD 21201
Phone: 410-767-7130
Website: www.dhr.state.md.us/blog

Massachusetts Department of Children and Families
24 Farnsworth Street
Boston, MA 02210
Phone: 617-348-8400
Website: www.mass.gov/eohhs/gov/departments/dcf

Michigan Department of Human Services
Department of Human Services
235 S. Grand Ave.
P.O. Box 30037
Lansing, MI 48909

Phone: 866-540-0008
Website: www.mi.gov/dhs/0,4562,7-124-60126---,00.html

Minnesota Department of Human Services
P.O. Box 64244
St. Paul, MN 55164-0244
Phone: 651-431-3830
Website: http://mn.gov/dhs

Missouri Department of Social Services
Broadway State Office Building
P.O. Box 1527
Jefferson City, MO 65102-1527
Phone: 573-751-4815
Website: www.dss.mo.gov/cd/fostercare

Mississippi Department of Human Services
750 N. State Street
Jackson, MS 39202
Phone: 601-359-4500
Website: www.mdhs.state.ms.us/fcs.html

Nebraska Division of Children and Family Services
P.O. Box 95026
Lincoln, NE 68509-5044
Phone: 402-471-9272
Website: http://dhhs.ne.gov/publichealth/Pages/chs_foc_focindex.aspx

Nevada Division of Child and Family Services
4126 Technology Way, 3rd Floor
Carson City, NV 89706
Phone: 775-684-4400
Website: http://dcfs.state.nv.us

New Hampshire Department of Health and Human Services
129 Pleasant Street
Concord, NH 03301-3852
Phone: 800-894-5533
Website: www.dhhs.nh.gov/dcyf/index.htm

New Jersey Department of Children and Families
20 West State Street, 4th Floor
P.O. Box 729
Trenton, NJ 08625-0729
Phone: 877-652-0729
Website: www.state.nj.us/dcf/index.shtml

New Mexico Children, Youth, and Families Department
P.O. Drawer 5160
Santé Fe, MN 87502-5160
Phone: 800-432-2075
Website: www.cyfd.org

New York Office of Children and Family Services
52 Washington Street
Renssleaer, NY 12144-2736
Phone: 518-473-7793
Website: http://ocfs.ny.gov/main

North Carolina Department of Health and Human Services
2001 Mail Service Center
Raleigh, NC 27699-2001
Phone: 919-855-4800
Website: www.ncdhhs.gov/childrenandyouth/index.htm

North Dakota Department of Children and Family Services
600 East Boulevard Avenue, Department 325
Bismarck, ND 58505-0250
Phone: 701-328-2316
Website: www.nd.gov/dhs/services/childfamily

Ohio Department of Jobs and Family Services
30 E. Broad Street, 32nd Floor
Columbus, OH 43215
Phone: 614-466-1213
Website: http://jfs.ohio.gov/ocomm_root/0002OurServices.stm

Oklahoma Division of Children and Family Services
Sequoyah Memorial Office Building
2400 N. Lincoln Blvd.
Oklahoma City, OK 73105
Phone: 405-552-1487
Website: www.okdhs.org

Oregon Department of Human Services
500 Summer Street NE E62
Salem, OR 97301-1067
Phone: 503-945-5944
Website: www.oregon.gov/DHS/children

Pennsylvania Department of Public Welfare
625 Forster Street
Harrisburg, PA 17120
Phone: 800-692-7462
Website: www.dpw.state.pa.us

Rhode Island Department of Human Services
Louis Pasteur Building #57
600 New London Avenue
Cranston, RI 02920
Phone: 401-462-2121
Website: www.dhs.ri.gov/tabid/142/default.aspx

South Carolina Department for Children and Families
P.O. Box 1520
Columbia, SC 29202-1520
Phone: 803-898-7601
Website: https://dss.sc.gov/content/customers/index.aspx

South Dakota Department of Social Services
700 Governors Drive
Pierre, SD 57501
Phone: 605-773-3165
Website: http://dss.sd.gov/cps/index.asp

Tennessee Department of Children's Services
Cordell Hull Building, 7th Floor
Nashville, TN 37243
Phone: 615-741-9701
Website: www.state.tn.us/youth

Texas Department of Family and Protective Services
701 W. 51st Street
Austin, TX 78751
Phone: 800-233-3405
Website: www.dfps.state.tx.us

Utah Department of Child and Family Services
195 North 1950 West
Salt Lake City, UT 84116
Phone: 801-538-4100
Website: www.dcfs.utah.gov

Vermont Department for Children and Families
103 South Main Street, 2 & 3 North
Waterbury, VT 05671-5500
Phone: 800-649-2642
Website: http://dcf.vermont.gov

Virginia Department of Social Services
801 E. Main Street
Richmond, VA 23219-2901
Phone: 800-468-8894
Website: www.dss.virginia.gov/family/fc/index.cgi

Washington Department of Social and Health Services
P.O. Box 45130
Olympia, WA 98504-5130
Phone: 800-737-0617
Website: www.dshs.wa.gov/ca/general/index.asp

West Virginia Children and Family Services
350 Capitol Street, Room 691
Charleston, WV 25301-3704
Phone: 304-558-3431
Website: www.wvdhhr.org/bcf/children_adult/foster

Wisconsin Department of Children and Families
201 East Washington Avenue, Second Floor
P.O. Box 8916
Madison, WI 53708-8916
Phone: 608-267-3905
Website: http://dcf.wisconsin.gov

Wyoming Department of Family Services
2451 Foothill Blvd., Suite 103
Rock Springs, WY 82901
Phone: 307-352-2509
Website: http://dfsweb.state.wy.us/protective-services/foster-care/index.
html

Foster Care Contact Information: Canada

Canadian Foster Family Association
www.canadianfosterfamilyassociation.ca

Alberta Foster Parent Association
www.afpaonline.com

British Columbia Federation of Foster Parent Associations
www.bcfosterparents.ca

Manitoba Foster Family Network
www.mffn.ca

New Brunswick Family and Community Services
www2.gnb.ca/content/gnb/en/departments/social_development.html

Newfoundland & Labrador Foster Families Association
www.nlffa.ca

Foster Parents Society of Ontario
www.fosterparentssociety.org

Fédération des familles d'accueil et ressources intermédiaires du Québec
www.ffariq.org

Saskatchewan Foster Families Association
www.sffa.sk.ca

Foster Family Coalition of the Northwest Territories
www.ffcnwt.com

Durham Foster Parent Association
www.durhamfpa.com/page/page/4711854.htm

Foster Care Contact Information: Australia

Australian Foster Care Association
www.fostercare.org.au/index.html

Foster Care Association New South Wales Inc.
http://fcansw.org.au

Foster Care Northern Territory
www.fostercarent.org.au

Foster Care Queensland
www.fcq.com.au

Connecting Foster Carers—SA Inc
http://cfc-sa.org.au

Foster Carer's Association of Tasmania Inc.
www.fcatas.org.au

Foster Care Association of Victoria Inc.
www.fcav.org

Foster Care Association of Western Australia Inc.
www.fcawa.com.au

The Foster Care Association of the ACT (Australian Capital Territory)
www.fcaact.org.au

Foster Care Contact Information: United Kingdom

BAAF (British Association of Adoption and Fostering)
www.baaf.org.uk

The Fostering Network
www.fostering.net

London office
87 Blackfriars Road
London SE1 8HA
Phone: 020 7620 6400
Fax: 020 7620 6401
Email: info@fostering.net

Cardiff office
1 Caspian Point
Pierhead Street
Cardiff Bay
CF10 4DQ
Phone: 029 2044 0940
Fax: 029 2044 0941
Email: wales@fostering.net

Glasgow office
Ingram House
2nd Floor
227 Ingram Street
Glasgow G1 1DA
Phone: 0141 204 1400
Fax: 0141 204 6588
Email: scotland@fostering.net

Belfast office
Unit 10
40 Montgomery Road
Belfast BT6 9HL
Phone: 028 9070 5056
Fax: 028 9079 9215
Email: ni@fostering.net

About the Author

Dr. John DeGarmo has been a foster parent since 2001, and he and his wife have had over 30 children come through their home. Dr. DeGarmo wrote his dissertation on fostering, entitled *Responding to the Needs of Foster Teens in a Rural School District*. He is a speaker and trainer on many topics about the foster care system, and travels across the nation delivering passionate, dynamic, energetic, and informative presentations. Dr. DeGarmo is the author of the highly inspirational and bestselling book *Fostering Love: One Foster Parent's Story*, a personal account of his experience as a foster parent. He also writes for a number of publications and newsletters, both here in the United States, and overseas. He is married to Dr. Kelly DeGarmo, and the two of them are the parents of six children, both biological and adopted. In his spare time, he enjoys gardening, traveling, and performing. He is currently located in the United States, in Georgia. Dr. DeGarmo can be contacted by email at drjohndegarmo@gmail, through his Facebook page, Dr. John DeGarmo, or at his website, www.drejohndegarmo.com.

Index